IN THE FACE OF DIFFERENCE

IN THE FACE OF DIFFERENCE

Congregations Building Understanding and Cooperation

William L. Sachs

An Alban Institute Book

ROWMAN & LITTLEFIELD
Lanham • Boulder • New York • London

Published by Rowman & Littlefield
A wholly owned subsidiary of The Rowman & Littlefield Publishing Group, Inc.
4501 Forbes Boulevard, Suite 200, Lanham, Maryland 20706
www.rowman.com

16 Carlisle Street, London W1D 3BT, United Kingdom

British Library Cataloguing in Publication Information Available

Library of Congress Cataloging-in-Publication Data

Sachs, William L., 1947–
In the face of difference : congregations building understanding and cooperation / William L. Sachs.
pages cm
Includes bibliographical references.
ISBN 978-1-56699-763-8 (cloth : alk. paper) — ISBN 978-1-56699-724-9 (pbk. : alk. paper) — ISBN 978-1-56699-725-6
1. Christianity and other religions—United States. 2. United States—Religion. 3. Religious pluralism—United States. 4. Religions. I. Title.
BR517.S23 2015
261.20973—dc23
2014026246

∞™ The paper used in this publication meets the minimum requirements of American National Standard for Information Sciences Permanence of Paper for Printed Library Materials, ANSI/NISO Z39.48-1992.

Printed in the United States of America

CONTENTS

Introduction: Between Ideals and Realities 1

1 What Would You Do? 7

2 Difference Hits Home 21

3 The Greatest Challenge 39

4 Images of the Other 59

5 The Challenge Congregations Must Face 77

6 When Fascination Replaces Fear 95

7 Mission and the Common Good 113

8 Leadership for Reconciliation 131

Bibliography 145

Notes 149

About the Author 153

Introduction

BETWEEN IDEALS AND REALITIES

There is a pervasive tension in American life. Among various sorts of tensions this is one of the most apparent. It permeates political conflicts. It fuels angry talk shows and blogs. It surfaces on editorial pages. More local than most sources of tension, it appears in ugly incidents across the country. It is more immediately religious than most public issues. It also taps some of the deepest American hopes, as well as religious ideals. It is an historic tension between ideal and reality. It is the deeply personal tension between wanting to welcome new people to our communities and fearing their presence will make our world unrecognizable.

The tension became apparent as a woman named Amy spoke of the West Coast suburb where she grew up. "In those days it was all Irish Catholic, or at least it seemed that way. Now it's Armenian or Indian or something. When I go back, I can't recognize where I was raised."

When pressed, Amy declared proudly that America should welcome all people. "That's who we are." At the same time, her sadness reveals a profound sense of dislocation. She has lost the place she once called home. She is proud America welcomes people from around the world. Her ancestors once were welcomed. But is there still a place for her? Can she find a place where she feels at home and where she will be welcome?

Opportunity is a prominent theme in American life. We pride ourselves on offering equal opportunity to all people, beginning with the opportunity to come to America and to flourish. At the same time we are sensitive, and even angry, at the thought that someone new and different would infringe upon our turf and change the world we have known. In theory we speak with pride of America's welcome to all. In practice, we speak of "immigration reform" and "cracking down" on "illegal aliens." American ideals can find troubling expression.

The issue is not confined to public debates or legislative maneuvers. It is not a creation of the media or an academic exercise. As Amy's wistful thought reveals, the issue is personal and local. People who are different have arrived nearby, and continue to come. They are drawn by our ideals, though they may not be prepared for our realities. As we shall see, the American population is more diverse than ever, and that diversity has spread across the nation. No longer just a phenomenon of large urban areas, diversity is readily glimpsed in small cities and towns. People of various religious and ethnic backgrounds can be seen in schools and in stores. They are at work in education, medical professions, and service industries.

In one small city, an aide in a nursing home was from Nigeria and her colleague from Jamaica. The young locksmith who came to open a jammed door was Israeli. At a convenience store, a Pakistani man sold bottled water. At a lunch counter, a Lebanese man described his new dental practice. On a bulletin board, a young woman from Honduras posted a sheet advertising her cleaning service. Next door, workers washed the large window of a new Thai restaurant. Such breadth of diversity now appears in every American community of any size.

Some Americans with a generation or more in the United States do feel troubled, even as they consider their own immigrant pasts, by the extent of immigration and social change today. But how might Americans as people of faith approach this situation, and the feelings it taps in them? More specifically, how might congregations respond? When an issue is intensely local, congregations sense it immediately. They are being redefined by it as well. Do congregations simply succumb to the issue's political dimensions, and thereby increase the tension?

In this book I describe the new reality of difference in the United States, and I chart a path toward faithful response by people in congregations. I will emphasize that difference is not only a local, social, and political challenge; difference is a religious challenge. Difference wears many human faces, and faithful attention to difference requires appreciation of the human dimension. This is the beginning of faithful response.

This is not to say that consideration of ethnic or racial or religious identity can be ignored. The reality of difference among people surfaces in such terms. The impact of difference reflects such human realities. A faithful response to difference can never gloss over obvious realities, but must engage them. We must not only see difference, we must see the humanity of people who embody difference. Learning to love one's neighbor, as all faiths urge, requires seeing the human reality that neighbor represents.

But, for all the similarities in theory, in practice religious faith is not an immediate solution to the challenge of difference. In many instances, religion represents the heart of the difference. As we shall discuss, the task of reconciling Christians and Muslims is the deepest aspect of the challenge. But various religious fault lines are apparent. The new ethnic and cultural diversity is emphatically a religious diversity as well.

If American, as well as religious, ideals and realities now are in conflict, what is the solution? For people of faith, the answer must be fleshed out in religious terms. These cannot remain abstract platitudes, but must be depicted in practical and local terms. This book does precisely that. It begins with an illustrative incident in one neighborhood to press the key question: what would you do? The discussion describes the new American religious pluralism in historical perspective to sharpen the question. The realities of Islam then show that the world's second largest religion faces challenges like those before American Christians and Jews.

The heart of the problem, we will see, surfaced in an incident broadcast on national television. A young woman was denied service in a shop because she wore a head scarf. How might congregations respond in their own situations when—not if—similar incidents occur? To answer that question, we will consider the challenge at the congregational level. What can be done in your local area? This question, and not abstract calculation, is the core challenge.

The answer is that we must return to the ideals of our faith. Surprisingly, we shall see, that entails practical response in terms of "mission." A central concept, especially for Christians and Muslims, mission actually is a call back to the essentials of faith in local and practical terms.

There is no glossing over the conflicts internal to congregations around mission today, especially with the array of tasks congregations face simply to stay afloat. But mission is the key not only to survival, but to faithful witness in the face of difference. In conclusion, then, I consider the task of adaptive leadership in response to changes of all sorts. Adaptation is the way to rediscover our religious ideals and to express them anew in life-giving ways.

In the course of this book, it becomes apparent that various conversations have shaped it. I am grateful to the people, all given pseudonyms, who appear on these pages. I am also grateful to the Alban Institute's publishing arm. In particular the friendship and encouragement of Jim Wind, now retired as Alban's president, reflects many years of conversation stretching back to graduate school. Richard Bass, Alban's director of publishing, has ably steered the book toward its appearance, for which I am thankful.

Various ties in my immediate vicinity shaped this work. I am profoundly grateful for the opportunity to serve St. Stephen's Episcopal Church, Richmond, Virginia, over many years. Most recently, thanks to the vision of its rector, Gary Jones, interfaith work has loomed large. The array of programs at the parish, bound by faithful education, worship, and pastoral care, make this an exceptional parish in which to serve.

The gift of such a broad horizon has fostered productive and enjoyable interfaith friendships across Richmond, Virginia. I am especially grateful for ties with Jewish and Muslim leaders represented by Rabbi Ben Romer, Imam Ammar Amonette, and Dr. Imad Damaj of the Virginia Muslim Coalition. I cannot think of them without smiling warmly and recalling countless instances of both honesty and friendship. I hope they see this book as an expression of appreciation for them.

Conversations with a colleague and friend, Dr. Aleta Richards, have been formative. Tapping her academic experience, she gave the manuscript a close read and formulated discussion questions and a study guide to extend it. Her various skills have sharpened the work. I am deeply grateful.

In an equally profound sense, the book has been shaped in conversation with HRH Prince Ghazi bin Muhammad of Jordan. His inspiring words, especially in his recent book, *Love in the Holy Qur'an*, would suffice. But his practical efforts to unite people of diverse faiths, especially Muslims and Christians, have been groundbreaking. In addition to leading the creation and publication of "A Common Word between Us and You," which we will consider, he has sparked Jordan's extensive efforts to honor the baptism site of Jesus.

For Prince Ghazi's efforts, and for repeated times of warm hospitality and probing conversation, I am deeply appreciative. This work is a token of that appreciation. From him I learned a valuable lesson: by God's grace, one can not only see difference, one can learn and grow from it. And one can relish the understanding and friendship it brings.

I

WHAT WOULD YOU DO?

THE DISCOVERY OF DIFFERENCE

Donna's phone rang often as the news spread through her neighborhood. A realtor had whispered what was happening and urged that the story be kept quiet. But the news was so alarming that it was soon widely known. Fear and fascination and worries about the impact on home values fueled conversation.

The word was that a Muslim family was moving into a house several doors away from Donna's. The callers knew these people were from somewhere in the Middle East. One thought they were Egyptian. As Donna first heard the news she began to ask herself what would become a nagging question: what should I do?

It was clear that the Muslim family had purchased the home of an elderly woman who had moved to a retirement community. Using yard and cleaning services, the woman had kept her property in good condition. As gossip intensified, cynical voices doubted that Muslims would be so clean. Some wondered if there would be multiple wives and if extended family would also reside there. In some neighbors' minds, a harem would arrive to serve an elderly, wealthy man.

Idle generalization was soon replaced by hysterical rumor. In one account the house would be occupied by a terrorist "sleeper" cell. All images of family must be a disguise for sinister intentions. Fears of terrorists soon competed with another rumor: the house would become a fundamentalist academy to indoctrinate neighborhood children with hatred for the United States. There would be aggressive efforts, and perhaps financial inducements, to lure children and adolescents as well. Islamic doctrine would mingle with extremist political ideas.

As fears escalated, some wanted to convene a special meeting of the neighborhood association. A few thought the police and their city council representative should be consulted. One person was certain that they should coordinate with Homeland Security. Calmer voices prevailed, and an anxious "wait and see" mood settled over the neighborhood. Telephone traffic slowed, but a few people still whispered in the nearby market. Several continued their dire predictions but agreed that the new occupants should arrive before vigilante deterrence swung into action.

As the neighborhood waited anxiously, Donna resolved that she would do something constructive. She was not sure what she thought of Muslims, and some of the dire predictions made her pause. But she concluded that whoever they were, she would find a way to welcome them. Typically she would bring a dinner or at least a cake or pie to new neighbors. She often gave them literature about area resources, especially museums, of which she was quite fond. Several times in the past she had invited new families to dinner when they had children near the ages of her own. She liked reaching out to new people because she remembered that when she and her family arrived, they had been welcomed. As a Christian, she felt a special responsibility to give back because she had received so generously.

This was not a casual thought for Donna. She and her husband, Ted, not only were active in their church, they had a profound faith. For them faith nurtured a responsibility to serve others. This meant helping people who were hungry and homeless, and so they regularly joined church groups to offer assistance. Service to others also meant visiting people in nursing homes and tutoring children with special needs. Donna had chaired several church committees and could articulate a compelling image of faithful people helping those in need.

Donna and Ted also discussed what their faith should mean at work and in their neighborhood. The instinct to help others remained strong for them. They agreed that simply trying to announce their faith, and perhaps pressure people to believe as they did, was wrong. But they were convinced that they should live as faithful people in all aspects of their lives. The pastor of their church taught that Christians witness to their faith by the character of their lives. Donna cited this point to Ted as she wondered what to do when a Muslim family moved into a nearby house. Should she welcome them just as she would welcome anyone else?

Donna had heard the rumors and doubted there was any truth to them. She had no patience with gossip. Still she hesitated. What should she do? They were Muslims, after all. There had not been a Muslim family in the neighborhood before. Maybe it would be better to "wait and see." But that did not seem good enough. Her faith would not let her off the hook and neither would Ted. "Okay," Ted said when Donna paused, "we really don't know anything about Muslims, just what we hear. And we don't know anything about these people. So what do we do as Christians?" Donna thought, and then quickly resolved to welcome the new family, just as she would welcome anyone else.

Still she hesitated. She admitted to herself that she knew nothing about Muslims and the culture they might come from. What if she said or did something offensive? She only had vague images of Muslims. What do they believe? What do they eat? Don't Muslims treat women differently? Maybe Ted should go instead of her. What could she read to be better informed? Uncertain about what to do, Donna was still sure she should do something. Then she remembered a church member who had traveled in the Middle East. She would call Bob and ask his advice.

Bob's response was helpful. "I want to welcome them, and usually would at least take a cake or a pie. But is that okay? Would they be offended? Should Ted go instead?" She felt awkward asking such questions. She also felt stupid about what she knew was a large, diverse religion. But no one else seemed to know. The least she could do was ask.

Bob reassured her. Pastries and sweets are readily served in the Middle East, he quickly said. If she avoided bringing pork or alcohol she should be fine. Encouraged, she baked her best cake and nervously walked down the street the day after she had seen the moving van. She hoped she could leave the cake with a note, but the door opened quickly. Inside she saw a smiling young woman in jeans and a sport shirt. Beside her were two young children in shorts and T-shirts. They began to chat, and soon Donna was inside and seated. In minutes they were discussing their families and local places to shop.

Donna readily accepted the offer of tea, and the conversation became warmer still. The conversation turned to schools and where a good dentist could be found. As they chatted, a man entered, and when he hugged the woman Donna knew it was her husband. He carried a laptop and wore khaki slacks and a sport coat. The man and the woman both spoke good English. As the conversation extended, both described college experience in the United States. Smiling and enjoying her new neighbors, Donna now dismissed all thoughts of extremism and violence.

The couple was indeed Muslim. They were young professional people who grasped the opportunity to leave an apartment in a large city for better living and less stressful jobs in a suburb of a medium-size city. There they hoped to have more time with their children and to become part of a neighborhood. They were aware the realtor may have talked and that there could be concerns about their religion and their Middle East heritage. But they were certain they could make friends and become a suburban family like any other. Donna's visit thrilled them. It confirmed their hopes. They simply wanted to be, and to have, good neighbors.

Soon they wanted to host a small dinner of nearby families. They wanted to show people they were a good family. They hoped their children could make good friends. They wanted to join local civic groups and do their share. Donna quickly described several such groups. As she did, one thought struck Donna: if I hadn't baked a cake and knocked on their door, I never would have seen what enjoyable people they are. They want to live like any other family here. Thank goodness I was able to welcome them.

More than ever, life in the United States is a matter of religious and cultural difference. And increasingly difference is apparent across the nation. Not only in the largest cities, but in medium and small ones, religious and cultural difference of unprecedented extent is apparent. North America is becoming more diverse, and this diversity is more spread out across the continent than ever before. And in unprecedented ways, difference is the subject of dispute. As we shall discuss, there is prejudice against various peoples, notably Muslims and Hispanics. Immigration has become a sensitive political issue. Fear of terrorism prompts suspicion of people who are different. The United States, a nation formed largely by immigrants, that has prided itself on its acceptance of others, now reveals alarming levels of fear and exclusion.

Where are America's congregations amid this troubling reality? We shall see that congregations share in the fear and prejudice. But even more apparent, congregations include people like Donna. In the face of what they hear and feel, they wonder what they should do. If it is wrong to endorse bias, then what should faithful people do? In this book I describe the shape of faithful response to the reality of religious difference across America today.

The goal of this book is to encourage understanding and cooperation amid difference that befits people of faith. Understanding and cooperation are the building blocks of reconciliation. This book points toward personal and shared reconciliation from a broad, Christian perspective. This means more than a sentiment; reconciliation means creating a capacity to live together in commitment to the well-being of all because of our own faith. Reconciliation does not mean dissolving difference, but living together in the midst of difference. I will maintain that this is possible only because of faith. We must understand one another on the basis of faith. In the midst of difference, even difference that has been accentuated by suspicion, there are life-giving touchstones, as Donna discovered. When we live deeply into our own faith tradition, we discover a basis for understanding and cooperation with other faiths.

In this new circumstance it is clear that older approaches to difference are inadequate, and a new approach on the basis of faith is needed, as the remainder of this chapter outlines. In chapter 2, I survey the new American religious pluralism in order to consider the situation of American congregations in the midst of it. For various reasons many congregations are preoccupied. There is a widespread inward turn and slight signs of understanding and engaging cultural and religious difference.

The greatest divide of all in the world today, as chapter 3 presents, is between Islam and Christianity. This is an historic tension between the world's two largest religions, both of which are growing. In the United States the issue cannot be avoided; largely by immigration, the Muslim population is growing. Understanding the basics of Islam is of crucial importance in itself. It also illustrates that in any situation where we have faced difference, getting an accurate understanding is crucial to moving beyond prejudice. Even more, understanding Muslim efforts to promote reconciliation offers a vital meeting point that must be appreciated and grasped.

As chapter 4 demonstrates, there is widespread prejudice. Sadly this is not new, as I explain. There is an extensive legacy of prejudice, much of it either directed at people of other faiths or justified on the basis of faith. Not all people give in to prejudice, of course. But there is a spectrum of response to difference by congregations. This chapter presents a typology of response that helps members of congregations to identify their own role in either endorsing or challenging prejudice against people who are different. Understanding how you have faced difference is crucial to becoming agents of reconciliation in your community.

Amid uncertainty and tension of historic proportions there is an opportunity that only congregations can properly grasp. As chapter 5 describes, this is not only an opportunity to promote Christian-Muslim understanding, as vital as that is. Overcoming suspicion and building reconciliation apply in a broad range of situations. These skills can enhance the ability of congregations to address various forms of difference, even those that divide them internally. The key step is to attend to religious difference, and to be willing to step beyond fearful assumptions. This means understanding how people who are different see God and believe God calls them to live their lives. Going outward, stepping into the life experience of others in appreciative ways, is the key to going inward and making our congregations and their local communities stronger.

It is possible to understand how another person sees God and sees the world and to build cooperation on that basis. Chapter 6 illustrates this prospect with reference to an impressive interfaith initiative in Omaha, Nebraska. Shared faith perspectives can be identified and translated into practical efforts. Across lines of difference it is possible to discern points of common affirmation and to work together.

Between Christians and Muslims, and people of other faiths and cultures, one issue consistently proves difficult to address. Christianity and Islam are missionary religions intent on making converts and remaking the world according to religious ideals. Both religions include energetic groups for whom competition and conversion are the only faithful options. In the search for understanding and cooperation, the meaning of mission must be addressed. Chapter 7 suggests that it entails proclamation of one's faith for the sake of the common good. Proclamation means being faithful in ways that avoid coercion and promote reconciliation to build better communities for all. America's congregations are crucial to making this happen.

Finally chapter 8 looks to the creation of reconciling leaders by faith communities. People of all faiths meet in the workplace, in schools, in civic groups, and in public places. Faith communities can encourage personal and shared vocation focused on reconciliation. Prejudice can be dispelled. Even more, hesitation to meet and to act can be overcome. With the right skills, people of faith and their congregations can leverage difference for the sake of the common good. There are varied examples from the past of how this has happened. It can happen again. Congregations can equip people to build understanding and cooperation again. For Christians this becomes a practical emphasis on reconciliation, as we now begin to explore.

OLD APPROACHES DON'T WORK

For various reasons, over many years, new people have regularly moved into American towns and neighborhoods. We naturally have been a restless, mobile people. Even if you have not moved for some years, you likely know people who have moved. And no doubt you have seen your neighborhood change. At the same time, America's schools and workplaces have welcomed new people and, in the process, faced difference. At times, all of us have been the ones who were different. North America has received immigrant groups for more than five centuries!

Difference has long been the reality for a nation whose ideals have emphasized freedom and welcome for all people. As the reality of difference in American life has become more apparent, a new word has been used more frequently: diversity. It has been an honored word representing a lofty goal. Befitting the many cultures that have found an American home, diversity has been affirmed broadly in public life, including in the churches where there has been much talk about diversity. Similar emphasis has been placed on being inclusive as well as being tolerant of difference. For many congregations this has been a priority, a reflection of the biblical emphasis on justice. Devoted clergy and lay leaders have pursued these goals as the core of their faith and their ministry.

But is this habitual emphasis on diversity sufficient now? Diversity, inclusion, and tolerance seem both noble and incomplete. Rhetorically they sound like first steps toward reconciliation. But in practice they are far from achieving it. Focusing on the business world, Martin Davidson makes this case in *The End of Diversity*.[1] Davidson maintains that "diversity" in practice has actually glossed over, and so dishonored, difference. Diversity has promoted an artificial picture of difference, but has failed to articulate how people who are different can actually understand and cooperate with one another. Diversity, as it has been pursued, would submerge difference. In practice this cannot work.

Instead Davidson sees strength, not division, in difference. Racial and cultural, as well as religious, difference embodies profoundly held values and perspectives. Tapping these differences in the right way, not glossing over them, can unlock deep potential for shared commitment. Thus Davidson emphasizes "leveraging difference" to both honor individuals and to enhance an organization's capacity for teamwork and shared purpose.

Of course Davidson writes of the business world and does not address the presence of cultural or religious difference in local American circumstances, as congregations reflect. For that matter he does not attend to religious difference except in passing and says nothing about religion's potential for fostering neighborhood cooperation. This is beyond his intention.

But Davidson makes a profoundly important point that has notable bearing on how congregations have seen themselves in relation to others in their local settings. "Diversity" has been a proud intention of many congregations. But what has "diversity" meant in practice? Often "diversity" has meant being welcoming to all. In part this has meant that a congregation would try to encompass diverse viewpoints, age groups, backgrounds, and races and cultures. More often than not a congregation is aware of whether it reflects the social makeup of its locality. It can also sense ways in which some groups have not been welcomed. "Diversity" has been an important intention by congregations committed to honoring all people in their setting. In this way the Christian image of reconciliation can take tangible form.

Even this noble goal has apparent limitations in practice. It is not enough to be welcoming when people approach a congregation. In what ways does a congregation address its context and with what intention? After people are welcomed to a congregation, what happens next? If congregations convene people more earnestly, what happens when they are convened? In many cases institutional process takes over. People are encouraged to become active by joining congregational committees. An ad hoc pattern of spiritual growth and leadership formation may also emerge.

Too often a person who proves reliable and likable will bounce from one program and event to the next. These may serve the immediate needs of the congregation, and the people involved may feel recognized and enlivened as a result. All too often the people who have become involved in this way can tire of committee service and the glow of spiritual energy can fade. Simply welcoming people for the sake of adding diversity to congregational life is an important step. But it raises more questions than it answers. It is not the end result.

This becomes clear when we consider that various intractable differences are apparent now. Simply inviting people to your congregation and placing them on a committee is like the habitual emphasis on diversity. It does not address the reality of difference. Unflinching religious and cultural difference is not engaged appropriately by diversity efforts. Many congregations have become all too aware of this fact. Over the past generation severe conflicts over theology and scriptural interpretation, liturgical change, women in ordained ministry, and, of course, human sexuality have wracked many congregations and their confessional traditions. Usually these differences have proven irresolvable, and in some cases breakaway congregations have organized like-minded affiliations. Diversity has proven to have jarring limits.

While congregations and denominations have been compelled to attend to internal fault lines, even larger social challenges have arisen. I will say more about these realities in the next chapter. For now it is sufficient to observe that diversity has been good up to a point. But the challenges congregations face now go beyond diversifying the people in the pew. Now congregations face the stiff challenge of addressing differences in the world just outside their doors. The dimensions of American pluralism have surpassed anything that diversity can adequately encompass, and certainly cannot resolve. Even more, an adequate response to this new situation must come in religious as well as institutional and social terms. But how can this be possible when religious and social difference frustrates efforts to achieve diversity? The pursuit of diversity is not an appropriate response to today's realities, within or without a congregation.

For Martin Davidson, speaking of the business and organizational realm, the way forward entails "leveraging difference." Davidson envisions an organizational process of team building that joins different values and perspectives for the sake of building shared purpose. I envision a similar possibility within congregations as they face their local settings. The greatest resource in this task will prove to be the faith that congregations hold. This is what sets them apart, and this is what gives them a key advantage to approaching people who are different because of their faith. Donna's uncertainty, and yet her sense that her faith should guide her, embodies both the challenge and the opportunity that America's congregations face.

AS A PERSON OF FAITH

Donna faced a situation that had sparked profound prejudice from her neighbors. For many Americans today, the reality of difference prompts prejudice that is actually the expression of fear. A natural human response to perceived threat, fear can also be a disproportionate response to threat that is only imagined. People and groups can be labeled in prejudicial, ill-informed ways. Groups that can be readily identified because of race or dress or religious and social practice may become scapegoats or, worse, they may be seen as sinister intruders who will wreak social havoc. When difference prompts fear, ill possibilities loom: at times anger and aggressive stances are apparent. Efforts to keep certain people out, or to defame certain religions cultures, may also arise.

At other times people refuse to accept difference and move away from it in search of situations where they deal only with those who resemble themselves. Pockets of the "like-minded" abound across our country. But the responses of either "fight" or "flight" lead only to frustration. Difference in the world, notably religious difference, is not erased, and the fears difference can induce are not resolved.

What is the relation between congregations and fear of difference? For all the emphasis on diversity that has been presented in many congregations, they can also serve as safe harbors where uncomfortable realities outside their doors are ignored or lamented. This can especially be true of contemporary religious and cultural pluralism. Though firm statistics are lacking, it would appear that few congregations engage today's religious variety. Few links are apparent between Christian congregations and Muslims, for example. This does not mean that congregations are always complicit in fomenting bias, or allowing it to spread. But it does point to the uncomfortable reality that this book addresses: on one of America's most challenging contemporary issues congregations are largely silent because they do not know what to do.

This paralysis reveals confusion about the religious ends and means appropriate to congregations. It also reveals that congregations fail to sense what they are uniquely positioned to do in regard to a crucial social reality. The result is that congregations are prone to allow fear to escalate, unless, like Donna, they consider the content of their faith and their vocation as faith communities. Then they become able to ask what they should do.

To do this faithful people as individuals and in congregations must see that they share in the fears of the people in their vicinity. But they must begin to distinguish themselves by asking what this fear is and what it means. They must discover again that fear in the face of difference is not simply a fear of extremism and violence. The encounter with difference taps anxieties about who one is and what one believes. Difference can lead to uncertainty and escalate into a feeling that the world is spinning out of control. Difference suggests that what one has valued and how one has lived may be lost. Difference hints that the familiar places of one's life will not remain the same. In a word, difference suggests impending loss. Indeed neighborhoods and towns and even entire cities can change. Change is a dreaded reality which many people and their congregations would rather forestall.

In this book I depict the life of faith as a journey toward deeper engagement with the reality of divine hope. I view this engagement as a literal and a symbolic journey invoking changes in one's physical and spiritual lives. The fruit of this change can be seen in deepening understanding and cooperation between people who are different from each other. Fear can subside, and the urge to control or to evade people who are different can fade. Interdependence can deepen, and trust can become one of life's most valued realities. In unanticipated ways, people who are different can enhance each other's lives, and together they can build stronger local communities.

The biblical basis for this hope is found first in Genesis 18:1–5, as we shall discuss in detail. For now it is sufficient to note that these verses describe how Abraham honors strangers who approach his tent by rushing to greet them. His hospitality contrasts with the intentions of the nearby Sodomites who demand that the same strangers be turned over to them for their abusive intentions. Instead Abraham prepares a feast for his guests. They prove to be angels who bring news that his wife Sarah will bear a son. The point is echoed in the Christian Bible, in Hebrews 13:2: "Do not forget to entertain strangers for by doing so some have entertained angels without knowing it."

At some point, amid contemporary American mobility and cultural and religious pluralism, each of us as faithful people, and the congregations where we gather, will face people who are strangers. How will we treat them? What does it mean to live as faithful people amid difference? It means to do as Donna did, conveying the example of Abraham and the words of Hebrews. She welcomed the stranger, greeting them and bringing food. Amid contemporary fears and uncertainties, this is the challenge faithful people must address. And this is the task to which this book is devoted.

QUESTIONS FOR DISCUSSION

When have you been a stranger in a neighborhood? Were you welcomed, tangibly as well as verbally? How?

How does your congregation welcome people? Would anyone find it difficult to feel at home in your congregation? If so, why?

How is your local congregation changing? How is it responding to change?

INDIVIDUAL AND GROUP EXERCISES

1. In what sort of community did you grow up? When did you first meet people who were different? What was your first response? How diverse is your current world?
2. Some groups of people are not as welcome as other groups in our congregations. Who is most welcome in your congregation? Who is least welcome? What do you think makes them less welcome? Use www.harvard.edu/implicit to help identify who and what makes you uncomfortable.
3. "Reconciliation does not mean dissolving difference, but living together in the midst of difference. This is possible only because of faith." What does this mean to you?
4. If we are able to welcome people who are different in our congregations, what's the next step? If we encourage them to join the congregation and take an active role, is that enough? What is "enough" when it comes to welcoming people?
5. How might you apply Martin Davidson's insights and his model in your congregation?

LEARNING FROM OTHER FAITHS

Judaism emphasizes the importance of doing. In other words, what one believes is important, but what one does on a daily basis is how one lives the faith. What can you do to increase understanding and cooperation and inclusion when you are in the face of difference?

SCRIPTURE LESSON

"'Do not let your hearts be troubled. Believe in God, believe also in me. In my Father's house there are many dwelling-places. If it were not so, would I have told you that I go to prepare a place for you? And if I go and prepare a place for you, I will come again and will take you to myself, so that where I am, there you may be also. And you know the way to the place where I am going.' Thomas said to him, 'Lord, we do not know where you are going. How can we know the way?' Jesus said to him, 'I am the way, and the truth, and the life. No one comes to the Father except through me.'" (John 14:1–6)

This passage is often recited at Christian funerals. It is a powerful means of assurance that the deceased person holds the promise of God's love for all time. Could this passage also be applied to the challenge of welcoming people who are different? Could the passage also be a means of drawing people who are different into constructive experience with one another? In other words, should Christians read the passage as exclusive, or inclusive?

PRAY

Pray for help in recognizing your fears and letting your faith guide your actions.

THINK ABOUT THIS DURING THE WEEK

The fruit of this change can be seen in deepening understanding and cooperation between people who are different from each other. Fear can subside, and the urge to control or to evade people who are different can fade. Interdependence can deepen, and trust can become one of life's most valued realities. In unanticipated ways, people who are different can enhance each other's lives, and together they can build stronger local communities.

2

DIFFERENCE HITS HOME

THE NEW RELIGIOUS PLURALISM

Whether you were alive then or not, you likely imagine the 1950s as a time of unity in American life. Television images portray the decade as a time of prosperity, unity, and integrity. Indeed, for much of the decade the economy was sound, and compared with the early twenty-first century prices were low. Despite fear of the Soviet Union and China—and communism generally—there was a broad sense of safety and trust. Major companies anchored the economy and American life and were presumed to be sound and to function in fair, moral ways. You could assume that with sufficient effort a job with a reputable company would be yours, and you would be set for life.

You could not imagine moving from where you were raised unless unusual opportunity arose. Nor could you envision much change in your hometown, even if you lived near a major city. You expected that your life and your community would remain much the same and that your sense of belonging and fitting in would endure. Certainly there was vice and crime, and there could be local tensions in your neighborhood and even in your home. But where you lived and how you lived seemed well defined. Major values and the public figures and institutions that embodied those values were trusted implicitly. American life was well defined and could be trusted, according to our images and memories of the mid-twentieth century.

Clearly America was a land of regional styles and accents, and local cultures. Life was different in big cities and their growing suburbs compared to rural areas in the plains or the western mountains. Southern states proudly spoke of a distinct heritage, while different backgrounds were apparent in the Northeast and the Midwest. But Americans pulled together, if memory proves accurate. There was pride in belonging to the local chapter of a national service organization, or in working for the local office of a national firm. As a young adult you joined organizations and built relationships you would keep for life. You started a family and a home, and you stayed put. You had a place where you were known and welcomed. You were at home. You belonged.

American religious life shared in this stable framework. There was variety in American religion, but there was a sense of all pulling together. Americans were Protestants, Catholics, or Jews. Discrimination against Catholics and Jews was receding; although African Americans continued to face historic prejudice, the first glimmers of a new day were appearing. Catholic Bishop Fulton Sheen became a popular television figure, explaining faith at a blackboard while dressed in clerical robes. He offered assurance in a way that was more broadly American than specifically Catholic. Religion and American life were aligned in a way that has had few parallels before and none since the 1950s. Though there was variety, religious life for the most part was organized along similar, institutional lines. In turn religious institutions received high levels of loyalty from their followers and widespread respect in public life. Religion reflected the institutional tone of American life generally and shared in the respect it received.

During the 1950s American congregations reflected the stability of institutional life. There were varieties of congregations in terms of size and location. To be sure congregations faced internal issues of mission, leadership, and funding. But belonging and believing were the backbones of American life, and membership in religious organizations had never been higher: nearly three-fourths of all Americans belonged to a religious organization, and most participated regularly and gave generously. Similarly, congregations served as local branches of large religious institutions in which they participated loyally. Americans worshiped and belonged in varied ways. But they felt their civic and religious values were secure.

Looking back, although the 1950s were a time of confidence, issues waited to be addressed, especially civil rights. Since then, religious America has changed decisively, though not in the ways many people assume. Religious America is different, and difference does not mean decline. Recent conflicts in religious life over beliefs and moral values, such as human sexuality, convince many people that the change in American religious life centers on conflict. Certainly many congregations can describe conflicts they have experienced over various issues, including leadership and overall direction. It would seem that the rise of conflict is the greatest change in American religion.

Any glance at church records will reveal that there has been difference among and within American religions. There has also been conflict of one sort or another, on and off, for years. At times conflict has even lead to church splits and breakaway groups. Disputes in churches in the 1950s touched many of the same issues that are now debated, especially what must be believed and what values must be taught. Media coverage was limited and communication was slower, perhaps making conflict appear less intense, and certainly less threatening to the social fabric.

But in one profound respect American religious life has changed decisively since the 1950s: what is called "pluralism" has increased dramatically, in ways that are unprecedented and could not have been anticipated. Just in the years since September 11, 2001, the presence of increased religious variety has become apparent. Religions that once were unknown to most Americans, or were far away, now are down the street. This is not only true in large cities; it is true in every city. A new, pervasive American religious pluralism has become unmistakable.

Through both personal experience and statistical data, Diana Eck depicted the changing religious profile in *A New Religious America*.[1] Eck shares her sense of discovery as she visits new temples and mosques across the United States. She pauses to remember her own Methodist upbringing in Montana and suggests she is still Methodist. But her religious framework has expanded as she has encountered unimagined variety.

America's religious pluralism is largely attributable to immigration. The United States has always been a nation of immigrants. But from the last quarter of the twentieth century onward, the extent of immigration has increased dramatically. By some accounts the foreign-born population of the nation tripled over the past four decades.[2] By 2010 more than 13 percent of the population was foreign-born, and perhaps a comparable number were the children of immigrants. From 2009 to 2010 alone the foreign-born population grew by over one million people.

Overwhelmingly, America's immigrants came from Latin America and Asia, with Mexico, China, and India as significant sources. One religion that has been in the media spotlight also grew noticeably, although its overall number remained no more than seven million, or a little over 2 percent of the population. Nearly two-thirds of Muslims in the United States came as immigrants and, significantly, they represented seventy-two countries. Immigration is as much of a challenge as it is an opportunity for religious life, and for Muslims the question is how one religious framework can encompass such difference.

Similarly, as many as 29 percent of America's forty-three million foreign-born residents, or over twelve million people, are from Mexico, with additional numbers from Central American countries. Notably the foreign-born segment of the American population has increased by 20 percent since 2005. Also noticeable, persons of Hispanic identity, whether born in the United States or not, represent over 16 percent of the population.[3] The religious impact of this growth has been most noticeable in the Roman Catholic Church and to a lesser extent in evangelical groups. Though statistics are inconclusive, some observers believe that Hispanic immigration has been the reason for Catholicism's net growth. Just as important, the Hispanic presence is having momentous impact on Catholic diocesan ministries and parish life as the church's historic profile shifts from Europe to Latin America.

The extent of immigration is unprecedented both in its variety and in its dispersal across the continent. As a result, an unprecedented projection is now possible in many metropolitan areas. By 2030, for example, when it is anticipated that about 1.5 million people will reside in metropolitan Richmond, Virginia, a majority of children born in the area will not be Caucasian; by 2047, when the area is expected to have about 1.7 million people, the region's population will have no predominant racial group; all will be minorities, as the *Richmond Times-Dispatch* reported on April 10, 2011.[4] Unprecedented difference, which is already apparent, is expected to increase to historic levels.

Immigration in general, and certain immigrant groups in particular, have aroused widespread public fears and levels of prejudice. "Illegal immigration" has become a political issue focused on Hispanic persons crossing America's southern border. The controversy gained momentum in 2010 when Arizona's legislature enacted a measure that required law enforcement officers to determine an individual's immigration status during a lawful stop. Criticism was widespread, and in 2012 the Supreme Court struck down aspects of the law. But its appearance and the debate that ensued pointed to widespread fears of difference.

These fears centered on dilution or even loss of historic American values and social ties. As proof, critics often cited the changing cultural shape of American communities. Different languages, dress, and cultural and religious practices became visible across the country. Various studies revealed that the overwhelming number of immigrants sought to absorb and sustain American values, especially America's emphasis on personal freedom. Akbar Ahmed's *Journey into America* described one after another local situation in which Muslims consistently endorsed American ideals. Yet Ahmed noted at various points that this represented a sea change from the America that was colonized largely by Europeans.

At the same time immigrants generally intend to preserve key religious and cultural beliefs from their pasts. Pride in their heritages blends with pride in being American. Nevertheless American life in general, and religious life in particular, appears to be shifting under new cultural influences. *Reflections*, the magazine of Yale Divinity School, devoted its fall 2012 issue to the question "Who Are We? America's Values Revisited."[5] Major voices such as Senator Chris Coons of Delaware, a Yale Divinity graduate, wrote to encourage reaffirmation of the role of faith traditions in America's political and social process. Other authors extolled the place of faith in sustaining such ideals as moral and spiritual development as a basis for citizenship, compassion in response to human need, environmental responsibility, and concern about excessive materialism and unrestrained economic pursuits.

The messages this issue conveyed were not surprising. But they were posed as being uncertain and needing reaffirmation in a nation whose demographic and religious profile is shifting. A general sense of recovering American values for a new era is apparent, and faith communities are a singular resource for society. At the same time, faith communities face the challenge of reaffirming their own historic beliefs and practices.

MEANWHILE, IN AMERICA'S CONGREGATIONS

If American fear of difference is intense, and perhaps even at record levels, what is happening in American congregations? Are they offering creative responses grounded in their faith traditions? Have they shown an ability to generate consensus that unites in the midst of difference? For the past half century, much attention has been paid to congregations, even by government leaders who speak of "faith-based" organizations and certainly by scholars of religion who have discovered the congregation's central role in American life. There is no more widespread grassroots organization than the congregation. It is the bulwark not only of faith traditions but of local life. How are congregations faring in the encounter with difference?

Despite signs of vitality and efforts to boost congregational life, signs of decline predominate, according to David Roozen. A Hartford Seminary researcher, Roozen has been in the forefront of Faith Communities Today (FACT), a massive, ongoing study of American faith, especially congregations. In "A Decade of Change in American Congregations," Roozen summarized a decade of study from 2000 to 2010.[6] He concluded that there was increased local initiative and greater spiritual energy. He could cite examples of innovative worship and creative reliance upon new electronic technologies. A general increase in the breadth and number of programs and initiatives was apparent. There were even examples of initiatives linking people and congregations across faith traditions. As you read and consider this chapter, it is likely that you can cite examples of these trends from your own experience of congregational life.

But there are also troubling signs from congregations. Roozen concludes that despite instances of vitality, the overall reality is a "slow erosion of the strength of America's congregations." He cites a high level of conflict in congregations, a steep drop in financial health, and aging memberships as general realities. Conflict has been the overwhelming reality, often fueled by financial and membership concerns. Studying over twenty-eight thousand congregations, Roozen concluded in 2010 that two out of three had experienced conflict in one or more of four key areas of congregational life—worship, finances, leadership, priorities—over the past five years. In one-third of these situations the conflict was serious enough that members left or withheld contributions, or a leader left.

A widespread effort is under way to define and to secure congregational vitality. Roozen and other researchers can identify the marks of vital congregations. They are more likely to have innovative worship and to develop "specialty programs" that appeal to particular audiences or needs, for example. Notably vital congregations may not completely avoid conflict. But they are better equipped to address conflict because, by some means or other, they have built a capacity to discuss sensitive issues and to discern ways to move forward that prove compelling for their members. Notably for our purposes, vital congregations are more likely to be engaged in interfaith efforts in their own contexts and beyond. The key to dealing with conflict appears to be a capacity to deal with difference, especially difference that has high-stakes significance and can readily alienate people from each other.

It is clear that conflict is unavoidable for congregations, and this is unsurprising. For a generation, news media coverage of religion has centered on conflict. Conflict seemingly arose over the activism of the civil rights era. It was not a simple matter of affirming or challenging equality for all Americans, especially African Americans, although this certainly was a factor. It was also a conflict over leadership goals and style, and the perception of some that church leaders had embraced particular political agendas. To others, eventually a clear majority in the churches, it was apparent that advocacy of equality had a religious mandate. Indeed the civil rights movement had unmistakable origins in the churches, where critical links were made between national-level ideals and contextual circumstances. The movement gained momentum as local leaders embraced it in their own circumstances.

In a number of Protestant denominations, the movement to ordain women followed a similar course. The admission of women to church offices that had been denied them reflected a new sense of the fullness of humanity and of the inherent sense of possibility that should be afforded all people. A deepening sense of ministry as vocation to which some people—women and men—are called took hold. The hesitation, and even opposition, of some in Protestant America eroded significantly, especially in the "mainstream" denominations.

But opposition to change, and to the activist style that fostered it, did not dissolve. In fact it coalesced into opposition groups, some of which eventually broke with their denominations to create alternative structures. Every congregation's members can likely describe tensions and even conflict leading to fracture. Not only have some congregations lost members over one or another issue, most congregations have experienced severe erosion of their ties to the judicatory and national structures of their denomination.

More than dispute over positions on one or another issue has been involved. Denominational structures have struggled to function as they envision they should for decades. They have seen themselves as centralized bodies charged with setting standards of belief and practice, guiding mission, and providing needed services. But congregations have increasingly been inclined to turn to independent sources and to cooperate with other congregations and service providers locally. The result is that, whether by choice or by circumstance, congregations face conflict and cannot presume that denominational resources can guide them through it. Denominations and their judicatories face conflict writ large and must navigate through it with diminished sources of support. As we shall see, the sheer existence of denominational structures can seem irrelevant or even a burden in the lives of many congregations. How denominational ties foster local vitality has become unclear.

It is certainly accurate to say that difference over human sexuality brought conflict in the churches to a head. In "mainstream denominations" debate over the place of lesbian, gay, bisexual, and transgendered (LGBT) persons, even the moral appropriateness of recognizing homosexuality became a firestorm. Two proposals generated heat and created fractures: first, to bless same-sex unions and even to speak of "marriage" in the church for LGBT couples; second, to ordain openly LGBT and partnered same-sex persons as clergy. In the Episcopal Church, the General Convention of 2003 confirmed the election of Gene Robinson as bishop of New Hampshire. Gay and partnered, Robinson entered the church's pivotal office and, in a sense, the core of its leadership. This step heartened many but infuriated almost as many. Americans, and the churches, were divided, and it was not clear how this severe difference would be resolved.

Homosexuality proved to be both a controversial issue in its own right and one which subsumed other, long-standing sources of conflict nationally and locally. For opponents it confirmed a long-standing conviction that church leadership had surrendered historic Christian beliefs and church standards in a race to be socially relevant. The move seemed an ill-calculated effort to gain public approval in a culture that had lost its moral compass. Rather than speak firmly and faithfully, the churches seemed to give in to popular sentiment.

Proponents of acceptance of LGBT persons remained steadfast in the conviction that they were expressing God's love for all people. They were hardly bending to culture, for the culture could readily exclude and demean LGBT people. Proponents believed the Gospel demands justice, which can be glimpsed as church structures change to embody the Kingdom of God. The Kingdom can never be realized on earth, but the church's manner and form can point to the eternal Kingdom which Christians anticipate by being faithful. Indeed fulfilling this sense of anticipation in its structures is the church's earthly purpose.

As a matter of dealing with difference, the conflict over human sexuality proves instructive. A decade after the Episcopal Church's consecration of an openly gay bishop, it was clear that the issue would not be resolved at denominational or judicatory levels. The issue would be addressed where religious America gathers—the pews of congregations. The ability of national church bodies to compel assent, much less provide crucial guidance to congregations, had eroded severely. At the same time, the conflict over human sexuality revealed the realities of congregational life that were gathered up by this sensitive issue.

Although sexuality is a profound issue with obvious capacity to divide, it actually taps still deeper issues in religious life, and especially in congregations. Conflict in congregations has more to do with fundamental differences over vision and direction, over control, and over leadership style than over sexuality or even belief. Finding resources and deciding how they are used often outweighs theological and moral fault lines. Cultural and social differences feed concern about the pastor's style and the direction of congregational life. In other words human sexuality is the perfect storm of an issue, gathering weakened denominational ties and uncertain local ends and means. In light of this complex, and far from alleviated, set of realities, it would seem that congregations have shown little capacity to deal with difference. In fact it would seem that congregations can be forgiven if most of their energies simply are used to ensure survival.

As if to make matters worse, a general erosion of American religion appears to be under way. As the *Christian Century* reported on October 31, 2012, the Pew Forum on Religion and Public Life announced that the number of Americans who say they have no religious affiliation has reached a record level—about one in every five adults now can be classified as "NONE." In addition, 6 percent of the population, or thirteen million people, now say they are atheists.[7] At the same time the Protestant proportion of the population has shrunk from 62 percent of the population in 1972 to 48 percent in 2012. Not only are the historic pillars of American religion eroding, more than ever religious America is defined by difference, including persons with no apparent religious affiliation.

Is difference the source of conflict in congregations? More likely it is the inability of a congregation's leaders to manage the differences accompanying change that triggers conflict. When conflict in congregations is considered closely, change of various sorts is the more likely source. Here change includes transitions in leadership, rises or falls in membership and finances, and changes in the context as well as in the internal life of the congregation. Conflict most often reflects inevitable changes or changes in the wider world. The issue is how congregations manage what is unavoidable, not whether change occurs.

If change cannot be avoided, neither can conflict. It is a natural aspect of life in human communities and organizations. It could be argued that one aspect of a vital congregation is its ability to face conflict. The measure of vitality here is adaptability: congregations must be able to adapt to change if they are to endure and to achieve vitality. It is clear that congregations where the basics are strong are able to face conflict, even beneficially. These basics are worship, pastoral care, education and formation, and mission/outreach. Where these elements are clear, done well, and offered in ways that people feel drawn into participation, then the congregation is well positioned to adapt to change and to see itself through the experience of conflict.

In one crucial aspect of religious life today I must be clear: it is sometimes thought that one or another sensitive issue—liturgical change, interpretation of the Bible, the ordination of women, or human sexuality—has ignited conflict in congregations. Persons who advocate views on one or another side of these issues can readily be accused of fostering conflict and even personally vilified. But such conflict is not simply foisted upon faithful people by malcontents of sinister intention. Rather people of good faith and worthy intention may see the world differently, especially on issues that are central to their faith lives. No bad motives or misguided perceptions may be involved or should be ascribed. Good people may see things differently and need not always agree. This is especially true in congregations where wider issues come to rest in local circumstances and interpersonal relations.

As a result, congregations face a myriad of differences today. The world they once inhabited, in which they felt confident about their identity, has vanished. A world of religious, cultural, and theological difference has arrived on top of the inevitable transitions that congregations have always faced. Difference is the reality that congregations must address, within and without. How well prepared are congregations for their encounters with difference?

CAN DIFFERENCE BE IGNORED?

It should be apparent that congregations of all sorts are well acquainted with difference. The sheer reality of conflict means that different styles, priorities, and visions of life surface in the same congregation. It is the rare congregation whose members cannot readily list issues that have divided them. But how well are congregations doing in facing difference? Just as important, how well do congregations face difference in the world just outside their doors? It may seem unnecessary to distinguish between the challenge of difference within the congregation and difference in the wider world. But in various ways many congregations do make this distinction, and they usually give preference to what happens within.

Instead, a key goal of congregational life should be to deal faithfully with difference externally as well as internally. This is a key message of this book. Unfortunately for many congregations today, this is a profound challenge. How your congregation deals with internal dynamics may differ from how it deals with external forces. Today there are signs that many congregations believe they can ignore difference as long as it is outside their doors. However, congregational vitality means facing difference well both within and without.

The trend to focus internally is not new. For decades it has been apparent that as a neighborhood changes, a congregation's members may move to other areas but continue to travel some distance for worship, meetings, and events. In one urban congregation, only members of long standing had keys to the building. The congregation functioned as a private club reserved for a few who had no relation and little interest in the world around them. Fortunately this was an extreme situation. But many congregations, especially in urban areas, can describe how they have distanced themselves from the surrounding world. They hoped to avoid change to preserve what they viewed as the precious identity of their local faith community. They did not want their congregation to be like the wider world. They wanted to preserve the essence of their faith and their fellowship. To do so they tried to distance themselves. They knew the world was becoming different, but they felt they could ignore it. Inevitably this proves to be a vain hope.

Yet this tendency to try to exclude whatever is different has become a widespread theme in American life. In his recent book, *The Big Sort: Why the Clustering of Like-Minded America Is Tearing Us Apart*,[8] Bill Bishop explains "why the clustering of like-minded America is tearing us apart." The firm divide between red states and blue states has been a striking aspect of recent national elections. But, assisted by sociologist Robert Cushing, Bishop finds that the problem runs deeper. "America (has become) a country of swelling cultural division, economic separation, and political polarization." Over the past generation Americans "have sorted themselves geographically, economically, and politically into like-minded communities."

Strikingly, America's congregations appear to share in this division; in fact, some embrace it. Homogeneity is prized. In religious terms this can seem like a necessary purity which sustains correct order and holds unfaithfulness at bay. The culture wars of recent religious life, notably over human sexuality, show the influence of this trend. But the net result is "economic inequality, cultural misunderstanding, political extremism, and legislative gridlock." Nor do these realities afflict the political realm alone. Divisions and even lawsuits among religious groups attest to the depth of the divide. Far from being needed centers of understanding and reconciliation, congregations can actually legitimate division.

But even when congregations do not actively foster division and eschew difference, they can participate in it passively. The examples of members driving through neighborhoods without engaging them constructively are common. Of course congregational leaders are not blind to this circumstance. They are aware that outside their doors are realities they do not engage well. They are also aware that those realities are changing, and that religious and cultural differences are the hallmarks of change in America. Today's congregational leaders may even be aware that eventually those realities will begin to redefine their task and their context. Still, many congregations and those who lead them persist in thinking that they must focus inward and can postpone or diminish the priority of looking outward. The sheer complexity of managing a congregation's life seems to demand this preoccupation.

Over the past generation the complexity of life within a congregation has come into focus, and not solely because of the level of conflict. The sheer dynamism of life in the congregation has become clear, and leadership strategies now can reflect the significance of dynamics that once proved elusive. "Polarity management," for example, poses basic sets of tensions as inherent and requiring balance.[9] Thriving congregations, for example, have both strong lay leadership and strong clergy leadership. Both have upsides and downsides; the key is to encourage one and diminish the other, seeking a healthy integration of the strengths of both. Similarly, "inreach and outreach" represent necessary polarities which vital congregations manage to balance. As a result, a congregation encourages creative integration of work within itself and initiatives beyond itself. Vitality is the result of balance between essential functions that might otherwise compete.

If "polarity management" poses the importance of a congregation going outside as well as inside itself, family systems theory speaks explicitly to the theme of difference in a particular way. Rooted in the work of Murray Bowen, and applied to congregations and other religious organizations by Edwin Friedman and Peter Steinke, this approach views the congregation as a kind of family system.[10] Congregations follow the dynamics of these intricate systems, even allowing for variations of size, setting, and spirituality. Particular dynamics come into play, notably anxiety, as the emotional processes of human relations unfold.

A powerful sense of belonging arises out of a basic need for identity and the clarity it requires. This need seems innate. As a result, congregations can promise assurance and stability of profound depth. But congregations also face life's dynamism, and anxiety can arrive as hints of change surface. Religious life itself promises movement, ideally from less to more desired modes of life and spiritual states. But the nature of religious life can conflict with the intention of finding congregational certainty. When change cannot be forestalled, and anxiety arises, conflict can arise in congregations just as it does in families. The prospect of difference does not appear to be welcomed.

However, the goal of family systems theory suggests a mode of leadership that can address difference in healthy ways. The ideal is to become "self-differentiated," that is, to be a person who remains connected to the system yet faces the anxiety of the moment and is able to change. Self-differentiated persons have less need for external approval. They cultivate a healthy dependence on others but can be focused and nonreactive at stressful times. Well grounded, this person can address the overall interests of a group.

As a leader, the self-differentiated person grasps key distinctions such as between facts and feelings. She does not demand that others be the same, but accepts differences between herself and others, knowing that differences alone do not cause conflict. She sees possibility and innovative goals, not hindrances or restrictions, in considering relations with people who may not have connected otherwise.

In a family-like system the self-differentiated person will likely face reactivity because she has implicitly challenged an unhealthy social network. Thus steps to accept difference are integral to creating a healthy, vital congregation. The leader taking such initiative must remain steadfast in being differentiated in this way. A core aspect of her stance will be to model such acceptance, because inevitably congregations face difference within and without their ranks.

Both polarity management and family systems theory illuminate key dynamics of a congregation's life. In its own way, each approach accepts the reality of difference and encourages facility in engaging it. But both approaches have shortcomings that limit their guidance in understanding and facing difference. The most obvious shortcoming concerns the religious nature of the congregation. Apart from broad references to its religious intent, the congregation is not depicted as a uniquely religious organization. Rather it appears as the analogue of other social institutions. This is helpful in revealing key dynamics.

The risk in applying these theories is that the religious content of key categories such as "mission" and "vocation" may be glossed over. The nature of difference in congregations and between people of faith is often over religious content and religious perceptions. Pluralism has expanded the range of difference and has seeped into congregations, challenging their capacity to address it. Understanding and engaging difference within and without the congregation is a religious task that must tap religious categories appreciatively.

In this chapter we have seen that congregations now face difference in new, multiple forms. Say "difference," and most leaders of congregations will think of the fault lines among their own pews, or straining relations in their judicatory and denomination. These sorts of differences are as easily enumerated as they are difficult to overcome: they are religious because they arise as fault lines over belief and practice, as well as the divergences over leadership and priorities I have noted. Such tensions within religious organizations have become all too familiar.

But other fault lines of difference begin outside the congregation's doors. The reality is that while congregations devote untold energies to resolving internal issues, they reserve little attention for the religious and cultural differences at their doorsteps. The result is that much of religious America is silent about differences that increasingly are shaping our world. At the same time religious America is unable to engage the underlying religious issues and can only speak of them in terms of organizational systems dynamics. The religious identity of the congregation, and the religious energies of our time, can be glossed over.

I believe that differences within the congregation are essentially religious differences, however susceptible they are to analysis by systems theories. That is, people readily differ over beliefs and practices, over the proper nature and source of authority for the religious life, and over the appropriate manner of life that follows from religious affiliation. "Self-differentiation" is helpful in pointing the way to acknowledging difference, but acknowledging is only the first step. How should religious people face religious difference in ways that are both effective and faithful? The question becomes acute when the difference involved seems to be a refutation of the very beliefs and practices one holds dear.

Even more, I believe that differences within the congregation cannot be segregated from differences without. Substantive attention to the religious dimensions of American religious pluralism and of congregational life is crucial to moving toward vitality. There can be no sharp distinctions between dynamics within and without the congregation. However helpful, theoretical approaches falter if they do not engage religious realities and if they do not point toward religious approaches to resolution. These realities are not isolated within congregations. A congregation inevitably is in dynamic relation to its context. The people in the pews of congregations inevitably live and move in wider circles. The congregation's boundaries are not firm, but porous. Religious vitality within a congregation cannot be achieved apart from vital, religious relations without.

This book explains what vitality means in the face of difference and charts a path to achieving it that is essentially religious. We will see that the core issue before congregations today is this: what does it mean to be a local faith community in vital relation to its context today? More precisely, how can a congregation proclaim its own faith in vital relation to a world of multiple faiths?

QUESTIONS FOR DISCUSSION

What signs of the new religious pluralism do you see in your own community? Where did you notice that new people and their religions are present? At work? In a public shopping area? At school?

In religious congregations with which you are familiar, does more energy go into addressing conflict or into promoting spiritual growth? What explains the emphasis you perceive?

What sorts of differences are apparent in the congregations you know best? Are these differences within the congregation linked in any way to differences in the local community outside the congregation?

How can a congregation proclaim its own faith in relation to a world of faiths?

This chapter focuses on the experience of white, Christian people. For them, the 1950s were dominated by European values and customs, which were very familiar and comfortable for them. What about people of color and non-Christian people? Were the 1950s a comfortable time for them? If not, why not?

C. S. Lewis said that many forms of worship are okay, as long as they are Holy. What does he mean? How does this apply to your church?

INDIVIDUAL AND GROUP EXERCISES

1. When was the last time you felt a sense of belonging? When was that in a congregation? When was the last time you felt you did not belong?
2. What have you noticed about church worship in recent years? How do you feel about changes in worship, or music? How do you feel about people wearing casual dress to church?
3. What causes bias? What forms does it take? Am I biased? Go to www.harvard.edu/implicit and take more tests to discover your unconscious bias.
4. What are some ways to help people feel they belong? In your congregation? At work? In the community?
5. Connections provide the security we need in the midst of change. Primarily this comes from our connection to God. Being human, we also need human connections; we need to feel that we belong. Given this psychological reality, how could your congregation make everyone feel more secure?

LEARNING FROM OTHER FAITHS

A famous American psychiatrist, Harry Stack Sullivan, said: "We are more simply human than otherwise." What does this mean to you in terms of your experience of other faiths?

SCRIPTURE LESSON

"But he . . . said unto Jesus, 'And who is my neighbor?' And Jesus answering said, 'A certain man went down from Jerusalem to Jericho, and fell among thieves, which stripped him of his raiment, and wounded him, and departed, leaving him half dead. And by chance there came down a certain priest that way: and when he saw him, he passed by on the other side. And likewise a Levite, when he was at the place, came and looked on him, and passed by on the other side. But a certain Samaritan, as he journeyed, came where he was: and when he saw him, he had compassion on him. And went to him, and bound up his wounds, pouring in oil and wine, and set him on his own beast, and brought him to an inn, and took care of him. And on the morrow when he departed, he took out two pence, and gave them to the host, and said unto him, Take care of him; and whatsoever thou spendest more, when I come again, I will repay thee. Which now of these three, thinkest thou, was neighbor unto him that fell among the thieves?' And he said, 'He that shewed mercy on him. Then said Jesus unto him, Go, and do thou likewise.'" (Luke 10:29–37)

PRAY

Pray for humility and compassion.

THINK ABOUT THIS DURING THE WEEK

In our global community, who is our neighbor? Given the limit on our resources, how many neighbors should we help?

3

THE GREATEST CHALLENGE

ISLAM IN FOCUS

Many members of congregations believe the greatest and most compelling differences they face are within, or spread across their own denominations. They may sense wider and deeper fault lines, but keeping up with immediate challenges can seem all-consuming. Precious little time is left for other considerations. But there is a greater challenge, and it is one that cannot be set aside. Increasingly congregations and their members encounter the religious pluralism that is a fact of American life. As they do so, congregations are forced to become clear about what they believe, what manner of life they encourage, and how they intend to build the good of the communities where they are located. Increasingly these core questions of congregational life cannot be addressed adequately without attention to today's religious pluralism. One religion has become emblematic of that pluralism and of the challenge of dealing with difference. In this chapter we consider the challenge of Islam.

There is no avoiding the presence of Islam. References to Islam have become a staple of daily news, typically in reports of violence fostered by extremist groups in various countries. In the wake of September 11, 2001, and the ensuing conflicts and fears of terrorism at home as well as abroad, American images of Islam are shrouded in dread and anger. A Gallup study released in 2011 revealed that nearly half of all Americans disapprove of Islam and fear Muslims. This is an extraordinary level of mistrust.

Yet Islam is the world's second largest religion, with more than 1.5 billion adherents. And its American footprint is growing, largely through immigration, and dispersing across the continent, as we have described. Islam epitomizes the challenge of religious difference and yet the necessity of engaging it. Like America's new religious pluralism generally, encounters with Islam now are unavoidable. What approach must congregations take?

I will use the example of Islam to describe how the best resource for engaging difference constructively is a congregation's faith. Religious difference must be understood and faced in religious terms. To do this, we begin by understanding the basics of Islam apart from the fears and assumptions that often surround it. The challenge is considerable. The differences between Islam and other religions, especially Christianity and Judaism, seem insurmountable. How can people of different faiths hope to cooperate when there is such a wide and historic gulf?

The path to cooperation begins with accurate understanding. But daunting questions must be addressed. How can one understand who Muslims are, what defines their way of life, and what they intend? Even more, how can America's Christian majority (over 75 percent of the population) understand not only Islam but the dramatic increase of religious pluralism in America? Where do Muslims fit in terms of the rapid spread of religious and cultural diversity? How do being religious and being American fit with one another today for Muslims?

The images associated with Islam are powerful and often negative. The growth of early Islam seemed defined by conquest, including repeated threats to Europe. Later Islam, centered on the Ottoman Empire, seemed marked by social decay and brutal rule. Modern Islam has seemed focused on fundamentalism and dictatorship. Of course Western images have been selective and have been touched by romanticism. The "Near East" has appeared as a land of mythical desert kingdoms defined by splendor and sophistication on the one hand, intrigue and rivalry on the other. More Western fables surround the "Near East" than any other region of the world. Images of castles, epic pursuits, romance, and the ultimate victory of truth and good surround Islamic culture. The *One Thousand and One Nights* collection of stories from Islamic culture long ago captured Western fascination. But such impressions add to our confusion. Which is the real Islam?

Memory has been the basis of approaching Islam for Jews and Christians. But memory has confusing and misleading dimensions. It blends past conflicts and grievances with romanticism. Fascination is a good thing when grounded in accurate memory. Remembering the past is key to building understanding and cooperation in the present. By remembering accurately we learn lessons and discover guidelines for living in the present together. It is important to consider that all faith communities use memories. But how do we use them? Does memory become a tool that divides or unites?

Because of complex past relations between Muslims, Christians, and Jews the task of remembering and using our memories is complicated. Inevitably memory includes past conflicts and past achievements, former grievances and affirmations. The task of remembering that is truly faithful includes recognizing the truth of the past—both good and bad; understanding the challenges of the present; and finding a common basis for respect and cooperation today. If Muslims, Christians, and Jews are to forge a shared future, they must engage memory properly in order to overcome conflict and draw on the ideals they share.

We begin to challenge false images and painful memories by understanding basic facts. What realities and trends define Islam today, and how do they compare with basic affirmations and trends faced by other faiths, nationally and locally, in congregations, where the life of faith is lived? How do Muslims tap their own memory to make sense of the present, and what might peoples of other faiths learn from their experience?

IDEALS AND REALITIES

The Five Pillars

If Christians and Jews are to deepen their appreciation of Islam, and extend the possibility of finding common ground, the Five Pillars are a natural starting point. They represent Islam's core convictions and point to the links between belief and practice for Muslims. It is also important to observe that for Islam, as for every religion, there are core ideals that believers struggle to express in the concrete circumstances of their lives. Every religion attempts to bridge the gulf between ideal and reality, but never with full success.

In part this is because religious precepts readily become entangled with cultural forms and practices. The interrelation of religion and culture is always complex and requires careful depiction. Religions come in various forms partly because different cultural situations have encouraged different forms of expression.

Similarly, when comparing two or more religions, one must take care to compare ideals to ideals and realities to realities. There is no more biased approach than to compare the ideals of one religion with the cultural and practical challenges faced by another religion. Understanding begins with identifying the ideals of a religion, then assessing how it responds to them. Thus we look at Islam first in terms of its ideals, expressed in the Five Pillars.[1]

1. Profession of Faith (Shahada)

Islam's core belief is easily expressed and understood: there is one God, and Muhammad is his prophet. Islam is rooted in these convictions. The revelations of God's nature and intention came to Muhammad over more than twenty years. Previously he had been a merchant in the city of Mecca on the Arabian peninsula. The revelations were recorded and later compiled in the document known as the Qur'an, Islam's sacred text. There is debate about what the Qur'an means for relations between Muslims, Christians, and Jews. But clearly there are various points at which the other Abrahamic faiths are praised.

2. Regular Prayer (Salat)

Muslims are enjoined to pray five times daily. The periods of prayer are generally not long, but the form is generally specified and involves ritual preparation such as washing as a sign of purification. Prayer may be done alone, but on Friday at midday prayer ideally occurs at a mosque in the company of others. Of course prayer at a mosque is encouraged whenever possible. On Fridays the midday prayers are more elaborate and include a sermon and perhaps an additional teaching by an imam, an educated member of the community who may have been trained as a religious leader and in some circumstances functions as a paid cleric equivalent to Christian and Jewish religious leaders. Typically, passages from the Qur'an and the sermon are in Arabic, and the mosque is usually oriented so worshippers face toward Mecca. Men often pray separately from women in spaces reserved for each at the mosque.

3. Fasting (Sawm)

Periods of fasting are enjoined on Muslims, the most extensive being the annual month of Ramadan, the ninth month in the annual Muslim calendar. For thirty days Muslims refrain from eating or drinking during daylight hours unless medical needs require it. The period of Ramadan is variable each year, depending on lunar cycles. It is intended to encourage patience, humility, and spirituality. Ramadan is also celebrated as the month of the first revelation to Muhammad. This time of fasting has a Christian equivalent in the season of Lent leading up to Easter. Though not strictly a fast, Lent is intended as a time of self-denial, reflection, and repentance. Ramadan concludes with a feast that in American cities has become an occasion for interfaith observances.

4. Charity (Zakat)

Derived from *Zakah*, the Qur'anic word for "purity," Zakat combines notions of charity, alms-giving, and a kind of tithe or tax. Though not always strictly enforced, it is strongly taught and encouraged. It is the principal way of linking religious observance to moral precept for Muslims. The giving of Zakat is intended to purify the giver and to alleviate the suffering of people in need. Spiritual benefit accrues to both, and society benefits as a whole both tangibly and from the moral example. Strictly defined, Zakat is 2.5 percent of one's worldly goods and is expected to be given each year. In this regard it is similar to the Christian ideal of the tithe, the gift of 10 percent of one's annual income for the support of the church and the benefit of those in need. As a result of the emphasis on Zakat, the Muslim world abounds in charitable organizations.

5. Pilgrimage (Hajj)

A ritual visit to Mecca is required of Muslims during their lives unless they are physically or financially unable to go. The Hajj occurs during a specified period of the year and the activities associated with it, including times of prayer and ritual walks around the "Kaaba," the black structure at the center of Mecca's holy square that Muslims honor as

Abraham's home. The activities of Hajj occur over several days and are prescribed in the company of other Muslims. Simple attire is specified. The occasion honors not only Abraham but the early years of Islam, and the activities of Muhammad in dislodging paganism from Mecca and restoring, as Muslims see it, the ancient faith of Abraham as directed in the revelations to the prophet.

The Five Pillars not only define Islam as a distinct religious identity. They also create a variety of parallels to Judaism and Christianity. Because Islam offers its own views of people and ideas central to the other two religions, the possibility of dispute becomes apparent. How differences can be addressed honestly, without diluting the faith of any of the three faiths yet seeking common bases for understanding and cooperation, is crucial. Of course, a similar task occurs within each faith, and even within congregations of the same faith, where internal differences can be prominent. In some respects, finding a common basis of faith is the hurdle that must be overcome.

For those who remain suspicious of Islam, one fact should be striking: certain terms or concepts associated with Islam in popular images are absent from this list. The most notable is jihad, which is often taken to mean "holy war" against "infidels" or non-Muslims. The term jihad is used almost daily in news reports and commentaries and is presumed to suggest that most Muslims are radicalized and prone to violence, especially against non-Muslims.

In fact the primary meaning of jihad is the inner, spiritual struggle of the individual to conform one's life to the will of God as revealed in the revelations recorded in the Qur'an. The will of God is primarily defined by the Five Pillars. A secondary meaning of jihad is a struggle to defend the faith in the face of external challenges from opponents. This sense arose during the early years of Muhammad's religious leadership when there was indeed organized opposition. Would-be contemporary radicals have altered these historic meanings, but the overwhelming majority of the world's Muslims adhere to the original meanings.

Similarly misunderstood, Sharia law is taken to prescribe a code of conduct that pits Muslims against other faiths and even is an affront to common moral values. To read much popular commentary, Sharia oppresses women, requires Muslims to act violently against non-Muslims, and generally assails Western notions of justice. Further, Sharia is both forced upon Muslims, the current myth maintains, and accepted without critical reflection by them.

In fact, Sharia, which can vary in content and application, is taken to be a way of structuring life along religious lines, much as canon law does in varying ways in various branches of Christianity. Sharia does not have an authority apart from the Qur'an, although it may be invoked in defense of cultural appropriations of Islamic ideals in some circumstances. Broadly, Sharia means a way of life and offers guidelines to being faithful. Islamic theological faculties may be called "Sharia institutes" as a way to denote that they teach the Islamic way of life first, and then as a legal code. In defiance of Western assumptions some "Sharia institutes" have women as a significant percentage of the student body and one faculty has a woman dean.

Less cited, but still controversial in the West, the term fatwa has been associated with extremism and violence. Some years ago an Islamic teacher issued a fatwa calling for the death of author Salman Rushdie after he published a book, *The Satanic Verses*, reportedly mocking the Qur'an and the prophet Muhammad. To some Western eyes, this fatwa confirmed that Islam is an intolerant faith that demands unquestioning obedience and is focused on violent suppression of dissent and difference.

In fact, a fatwa is an opinion that any Muslim can issue. Certainly noted teachers and public figures command more attention and likely greater response. But one fatwa from one source could hardly be taken as representative of Islam as a whole, just as the intention of one Christian preacher to burn the Qur'an would not be representative of Christians as a whole. Major Muslim teachers note that a fatwa is an opinion, typically issued in reply to an individual's question about particular aspects of religious practice, centering on prayer, dress, fasting, charity, and so forth. In most cases, there is little capacity to enforce a fatwa. Christian and Jewish clergy also issue opinions, especially in sermons, with similarly little capacity to enforce them.

Like a sermon, the fatwa rests on an ability to be persuasive. Islam, like Judaism and Christianity, rests on consensus, and on whether one interpretation proves more compelling than another. Of course, family or community pressure for a particular view can be compelling. But Islam, like other religions, takes shape in cultural and social settings where the line between religion and context can be obscure. The values of both flow into each other. Religion, after all, is an effort to organize life according to certain ideals in the midst of specific circumstances. Religion shapes life, and is shaped by it. Understanding another religion entails seeing how its ideals have given rise to ways of life in multitudes of settings.

KEY TRENDS OF MUSLIM LIFE

On close examination more complex realities define the Muslim world than fundamentalism or extremism. It is also clear that these realities reflect challenges faced by other religions. While these realities contribute to extremism in some instances, more often they fuel quite different religious and social movements, including various forms of spirituality and debate over the meaning of democracy. Five trends define Islam today. As we consider each, think of how these trends may also be impacting your own faith and the life of your congregation.

1. Youth

Predominantly Muslim nations are among the world's youngest. Consider the following statistics from countries that are prominent in today's news:

Egypt has a population of eighty-three million, with a median age of twenty-four;
Jordan has a population of 6.5 million with a median age of twenty-four;
Libya has a population of 6.3 million with a median age of twenty-three;
Oman has a population of three million with a median age of eighteen;
Turkey has a population of seventy-seven million with a median age of twenty-seven.

Other large countries that are predominantly Islamic reflect the trend to a youthful population. Indonesia, the world's largest Muslim country, had 237 million citizens and a median age of twenty-eight in early 2011. The average age of first marriage was 19.8. In Pakistan the population reached 180 million in 2011 with a median age of 21.6. By contrast, in early 2011 the United States had a population of 310 million with a median age of thirty-seven. In Great Britain the population was nearly sixty-two million and the median age was nearly thirty-nine.[2]

What accounts for the youthful population of the Muslim world? The obvious answer is that there has been improved health care, especially in nations with more resources and higher education levels. There has been emphasis on medical science, which finds its roots in Islam and the Islamic world's intellectual standing from medieval times. Also there is long-standing emphasis on the family and on the ties of extended families. Children are loved and honored in every faith and culture. But in many parts of the Muslim world there has been dramatic growth, making young people valued. Yet population growth strains health care and educational resources, and young people have difficulty finding jobs after their education.

2. Education

No aspect of life is more prized, or more the subject of frustration in the Muslim world, than education. Islam's sense of itself includes powerful images of learning and great centers of education. Indeed the world's oldest university is Al Azhar in Cairo, a huge, influential center of learning. Islamic scholars in the Middle Ages preserved ancient Greek and Roman learning and created a new synthesis of faith and inquiry. Education has been the defining feature of Islamic life after the central focus on regular prayer. Today many colleges and universities in Islamic cultures make fresh efforts to unite faith and knowledge, especially in the sciences. New centers of learning are emerging, and in some nations the level of education is high.

But access to education can be difficult. Hunger for education is great, but there are not enough places for students who wish to attend. One North African school had over twenty thousand applications for three hundred spots in an entering class. Worse, chronic poverty prevents many from even applying. For those who are admitted and receive diplomas and degrees, there may not be job opportunities. Given the strained global economy, many aspiring and even successful students find it difficult to gain and utilize an education. One of the greatest sources of frustration among youthful Muslim populations is the lack of opportunities related to education.

In part the education gap in some countries has been addressed by the rise of madrassas, or conservative Islamic schools. These schools have been called breeding grounds for extremism and to a small degree that has been true. For the most part madrassas are like Bible schools in conservative Christian circles: they require students to memorize the Qur'an, without analysis of it. Such an approach hardly prepares students to grasp their faith or to find jobs.

3. Women

One of the most controversial aspects of Muslim life concerns the status of women. A few authors cite their painful personal experiences to imply that all Muslim women are more or less oppressed, and some non-Muslims readily echo this view. In addition, non-Muslims sense restrictions on women that seem inherent in Islamic life. In reply Muslims cite the Qur'an to show there is no inherent repression of women. Patterns of dress and family relations reflect both patterns of piety and important distinctions of role. Of course, dress and family ties also are as rooted in culture, and cultural views of faith, as they are in Islam itself.

Religion and culture often blend in ways that appear seamless. It can be difficult to distinguish what is truly one or the other. Christians and Jews can easily think of examples of culture and religion blending in ways that are both influential and confused.

On close examination one discovers not only that the status of women varies from one culture and country to the next, but that the circumstances of women can challenge negative stereotypes. This is especially true in politics. Two Muslim nations, Pakistan and Turkey, have had women as prime ministers. In another nation, Bangladesh, two women have been leading political rivals for years. Women increasingly hold cabinet and diplomatic posts, and other key political roles. Sallama Shaker of Egypt has been her country's ambassador to Canada after a long diplomatic career including time as deputy foreign minister.

Women are prominent in professional life. In some countries, many medical students are women. Women with specialized professional and technical skills are more visible than ever. Just as in the Western world, opportunities for women are expanding. In some cases women are even the majority of students in Islamic theological schools. In Qatar, a woman is the dean of a theological institute affiliated with a major university. For every generalization that has been made about the status of women in the Islamic world, more exceptions can be found.

4. Spirituality

Upsurges in personal spirituality are prominent in the Muslim world and represent important parallels to trends among Jews and Christians. In the Western world there has been much notice of young women wearing head scarves, an image that has tapped latent fear and prejudice. In both predominantly Muslim settings, and where Muslims are a minority, more young women are wearing the head scarf by choice, as a sign of religious devotion. Muslim student groups are more visible on American campuses, and more Muslims are observant of particular periods of prayer and fasting.

This is hardly the first time in Islam's history that there has been a widespread surge of spirituality with no sinister implications. A variety of groups and styles from the past continue to illustrate Islam's significant and varied spirituality. The greatest influence has been that of Sufism, a broad legacy of prayer and devotion. More recently, in the twentieth century, a renewal of personal devotion and evangelism centered on men arose in India. Called "TablighiJamaat," or "Society for Spreading Faith," it calls for increased devotion with emphasis on evangelism and fellowship. TablighiJamaat encourages a calm, contemplative nature and empowers followers to rouse fellow Muslims from half-hearted faith.

The examples could be multiplied, and few suggest extremism or opposition to people of other faiths. Of course, a powerful and much discussed influence among Muslims arose with the Wahabi movement in what is now Saudi Arabia in the eighteenth century. A curious parallel to the rise of Evangelicalism in Britain and North America, Wahabism has similarly been the source of strict moral teaching and zeal to bring as many people as possible to literal belief and interpretation of scripture. Like Evangelicalism, Wahabism has been the source of religious fundamentalism since the twentieth century.

For all the memories of past spiritual movements among Muslims, today there is a difference, and it also parallels trends among Christians and Jews. Today the Muslim world is noted for independent groups and self-appointed leaders. Apart from the influence asserted by individual governments, Islam is a highly decentralized religion. It is not only divided into Sunni and Shia, but into subgroups, movements, and sects of varying description. Add the varieties of race and culture, and one sees the Islamic world in its true light: a faith that is both visible and united in basic precepts, and fragmented in its linkages and loyalties.

5. Reform

From the Western world's perspective, fundamentalism and extremism appear to dominate Muslim life. Some non-Muslim Americans wonder when so-called "moderate Muslims" are going to "stand up" to refute the extremists. A few Western scholars believe that something "went wrong" in Muslim societies. Even informed voices have argued that the Islamic world has been in decline, that Islam is prone to extremism, and that would-be reformers face daunting challenges if they are to be heeded. It has been a widespread assumption, one that feeds prejudice, that Islam is immune to reform.

With the rise of movements for democratic reform in several Middle Eastern countries, it should now be clear that the Islamic world has hardly been quiet. Far from images of repression to which most Muslims give in, energetic conversations about faith and public life have taken shape. These impulses hardly play into the hands of extremist minorities. Instead, in varying ways in different countries, increasing segments of the population reject extremism in both religious and political terms and seek societies that are both faithful and democratic.

In part the movement for reform has economic sources. The global recession has been severe in some places. Libya, for example, has had a 30 percent unemployment rate, while Turkey has reported 15.5 percent and Egypt nearly 10 percent. These figures do not reflect the extent to which people are underemployed or employed for wages that cannot sustain one's life much less the life of a family. They become alarming figures when one considers the extent of education in various countries. Much of a generation of young people feels its future is threatened and blames governments that it deems corrupt and inefficient. It is also notable that young women are active in reform movements in the Islamic world. It is not surprising that would-be reformers see their intentions in religious as well as political and economic terms. The trends defining Islamic life cross-fertilize, with an emphasis on democratic reform being the most prominent.

Cynics may insist that Islam has sorely needed reform. Lingering suspicions of Islam cluster around treatment of women, intellectual freedom, and human rights in general. Though challenges of Islam on specific aspects of these themes can be telling, other religions and cultures are not exempt from similar critiques. Every religion has had to confront its own legacies in light of fresh perspectives on revealed truth. Reform is a mark of a vibrant faith seeking fresh expression of eternal truth. In that regard Islam proves itself to be dynamic, varied, and changing in ways that suggest fresh cooperation with others.

A CONFLICTED HISTORY

Many American Christians today regard Islam as inherently violent. Tension in the Middle East and the association of Islam with terrorist groups have left a deep impression. Even more charitable American opinion fears that Islam lacks sufficient ability to control its extremes. "When are the moderate Muslims going to stand up?" has been a frequent question in discussions of the Abrahamic faiths. Islam appears more prone to violence than other faiths, partly because it seems unable to restrain the extremists in its midst.

In other contexts and other parts of the world the images are reversed. Instead of Muslims being prone to violence and lacking control of their ranks, it becomes Jews or Christians who represent danger and who cannot reign in their violent colleagues. Muslims may cite the American invasion of Iraq, linking it to the Crusades of centuries ago, and note the influence of evangelical Christians on American foreign policy. Muslims may also critique American support of Israel, including its repeated transfers of sophisticated weapons and reluctance to oppose Israeli settlers who claim Palestinian land as their own. Land deemed sacred can seem violated if "the other" is present, or worse, has political control over it.

Jews, on the other hand, still reeling from the Holocaust, doubt that they can fully trust any other faith or nationality. Repeatedly victimized, at times savagely, many Jews have resolved to define their own future and to defend their religious sense of destiny. Most Jews readily acknowledge the extremist impulses in their own ranks, but they are slow to criticize lest their unity be weakened. Unity is necessary if one's survival is at stake.

We should never be quick to judge another person's perceptions, especially if survival is the issue. Jews have the long memory of being largely excluded from their ancestral land after the Roman Empire destroyed Jerusalem in 70 BCE. Only a remnant could stay, and they were subject to the control of others, at times violently. But all three of the Abrahamic faiths can point the finger at the others and accuse them of hateful intentions. Christians can be quick to speak of Muslim armies advancing on Europe from the east and the west centuries ago, and to see Muslim immigration to Europe today as a modern form of invasion. Memories of ancient battles become heroic attempts to save Europe for the true faith and to repel the evil invader, when the reality was more complex. What if Oxford had become a Muslim university? historian Edward Gibbon once wondered. In the popular imagination today, the same fear is apparent.

Muslims could respond that the Crusades in the Middle Ages were more deadly and more purely religious in their motivation. The goal, of course, was for Christians to reclaim the holy land for the true faith from the false faiths. If Muslims seemed to advance on Europe at different times from different directions, Christians assaulted Muslims and Jews in the Middle East repeatedly over several hundred years. In Muslim eyes, the heroic leader Saladdin blunted crusading armies but refused to slaughter Christians or Jews he captured. Indeed, he refused to claim holy places of these faiths for Islam. To Muslims, this great general not only defended holy places, he displayed Islam's respectful nature.

Images of cruelty and heroism vary depending on the perspective of one's faith. Each faith can slide into a sense of entitlement and victimhood, its own triumphalism and destiny and self-justification. Each faith can turn exclusive and inflexible.

Of course conflict that seems generated by religious convictions and resentments may actually be economic, social, or political, or may simply represent ambitions and rivalries cloaked in religious categories. The division of the Middle East along national boundaries took shape after World War I because of British and French power objectives. During the war itself Germany had tried to rouse Muslims to holy war against Britain and France without success. Cynically, Germany had assumed that Muslims carried resentments and were prone to a violence that could be enlisted. But hordes of bloodthirsty Muslims never materialized. Whatever their sense of grievance, most Muslims were aware they were being manipulated and were not prone to see a proxy role in a war between European powers as the highest expression of their faith.

The sense of danger from the other faiths is high for each of the Abrahamic religions. It does little good to dwell on political and economic factors; they absorb religious energies and arouse religious hopes and grievances. But faith can gather up various realities and dramatize them in uniquely powerful ways. For countless people, faith is the defining reality in their lives. What matters most is what you believe and how you live because of your beliefs. Yet the blend of faith with other realities becomes murky. Often there is no purely religious motivation apart from the realities of one's social context.

For all people of faith, core questions then surface and must be addressed in terms of the situations they face. For example, how does your faith teach you to live, to what patterns of life are you called, and what must you avoid? Above all, what does your faith teach you to be when you encounter people of other faiths, especially when you believe your faith has an historic grievance against another faith? What does it mean to be a follower of one faith when you live in the midst of other faiths? Does your faith motivate you to oppose the other faiths, passively or aggressively? Or is there some basis in your faith that allows, and maybe affirms, living peacefully with religious difference?

A segment of the Muslim leadership has grasped the challenge of overcoming difference. In the fall of 2007, a remarkable document called "A Common Word between Us and You" appeared.[3] This was an open letter from the Muslim world to the Christian world. Its intention was to elicit widespread recognition that the world's two largest religions share the same core convictions: there is one God, and believers are called to love God and their neighbor. As Matthew 22:40 in the

Christian Bible records, quoting Jesus, "on these two commandments hang all the law and the prophets."

Response to "A Common Word" has been extraordinary. Over three hundred Muslim leaders and over five hundred Christian leaders have endorsed the document. Several conferences at major academic institutions in the United States and Britain have brought together disparate leaders. Jewish leaders, sensing that they shared the ideals and intentions of the letter, have also been involved. The hope has been that something of a movement could be launched, drawing together the vast majority of the people of the Abrahamic faiths in goodwill and common hope.

In light of "A Common Word," it is clear that the Abrahamic faiths reflect very similar sorts of memory. In all three particular persons and events frame the core beliefs of one God and love of one's neighbor. All three emphasize revelation, that is, special expressions of God's nature, intention, and involvement in human life. Some of the very same persons are honored: we speak of the "Abrahamic" faiths because the ancient patriarch Abraham is revered by all. But these similarities soon become less certain. Christians and Muslims join Jews in honoring Moses, who led the ancient Hebrew people out of Egypt toward a promised land. Others of the ancient prophets, such as Elijah, are honored as well. But when one looks at how these historic figures are understood and honored, one begins to see the differences between the faiths.

Take Abraham, for example. Muslims understand the Kaaba in Mecca, Islam's historic home and symbolic center, to have once been Abraham's home. But this view is absent from Judaism and Christianity. For that matter, the Muslim sacred text, the Qur'an, honors Christians, honors Jesus, and even cites the Virgin Mary, Jesus's mother. But Christians center their faith on an affirmation of Jesus as the Son of God, that is, God in human form, while Muslims honor Jesus as a prophet, a precursor—perhaps the greatest precursor—to the revelation expressed through the prophet Muhammad. The notion that Jesus was God's son challenges the monotheism that is Islam's cornerstone. Similarly, Jews reject Jesus and his followers, especially Paul, as a fracture of the covenant God made with the people of Israel, rather than a reframing of that covenant.

The city of Jerusalem dramatizes the commonalities and divergences of the three faiths. At the same time, Jerusalem is the site of Israel's historic temple, the locus of Christianity's understanding of Jesus's death and resurrection, and the site of the prophet Muhammad's journey to heaven. Thus the city has powerfully symbolic and historic qualities, but in divergent ways. It is a profound, living illustration of how the ideals and realities of different faiths need not collide; in skillful hands, they can be expressed in ways that invite mutual affirmation.

The ideals of one faith can align with the ideals of another in surprising ways; similarly, comparison of the challenges faced by one faith likely will surface analogous challenges in the other faith. The task of promoting interfaith understanding and cooperation centers on affirming the similarities, appreciating the differences, and building respect in the process. The challenge is to stand on one's own ground and to grasp that others must stand on theirs. From each perspective, intersections can be identified and can become the basis of cooperation.

"A Common Word" lifts up two basic tenets of Islam and Christianity that also resonate closely with Judaism. But how closely could these affirmations draw you toward people of the other two faiths? The answer is that we can go a lot farther than is generally assumed in making common affirmation and in facing common challenges. The differences between the faiths are genuine, but so are the similarities of belief and practice and so are contemporary challenges. How can we emphasize these parallels to enhance our capacity to understand one another?

"A Common Word" declares that there is one God, and God teaches love of one's neighbor. We have gotten a glimpse of Islam's approach to these ideals, and we have noted Islam's origin, variety, and growth. Now let us suggest that aspects of Islam in practice open up further dimensions of common affirmation. All three religions emphasize qualities of life lived faithfully that could extend the word we share in common and bridge perceived differences. But this sense of possibility must be realized in the complex encounters of American religious pluralism. Difference, however historic, must be overcome in terms of the present.

QUESTIONS FOR DISCUSSION

1. As you consider the basic ideals of Islam as outlined here, what favorable comparisons do you find with Christianity or Judaism? What trends are similar among the three religions?

2. Sometimes we lean into the known or the absolute because it's more comfortable. It is easier than struggling with ambiguity. We know there are absolutes in matters of faith, but there also are "gray areas" which resist certainty, and when we must struggle to find the right course of action. What are some of these situations?
3. What do you do when you are uncertain what is the right thing? Do you consult anyone?
4. How does prayer help you to know what to do?

INDIVIDUAL AND GROUP EXERCISES

1. What faith group other than Islam seems really different to you? Do you know enough about Islam to identify common affirmations and common challenges? What could you do to learn more?
2. The Five Pillars of Islam are described in this chapter. What would you say are the pillars of Christianity? Of Judaism? How do you as a person of faith live the basic affirmations of your faith?
3. Identify the myths Christians have about other faiths, and people of other faiths have about Christianity.
4. Read "A Common Word." What do you think about it? If asked to write your own "common word," what would you propose?
5. Is love of God and love of neighbor the core of faith? What is the most important message of faith in your experience?

LEARNING FROM OTHER FAITHS

Have you ever read the sacred text of another faith? What did you learn about values, about personal responsibility, about making decisions?

SCRIPTURE LESSON

"Give your servant therefore an understanding mind to govern your people, able to discern between good and evil; for who can govern this your great people?" (1 Kings 3:9)

The process of making decisions involves discernment, sometimes struggling with what is right and wrong in a given situation. Even Solomon asked God for help. What do you think about 1 Kings 3:9?

PRAY

This week, pray for the ability to love those who are different.

THINK ABOUT THIS DURING THE WEEK

Moses was given Ten Commandments. Why did Jesus focus on love of God and love of neighbor?

4

IMAGES OF THE OTHER

THE OTHER IN AMERICA TODAY

A Revealing Incident

Several years ago a major television network, ABC News, broadcast a notable experiment. As part of its "What Would You Do?" series, ABC sent a young woman who apparently was Muslim into a Texas neighborhood bakery. Wearing a head scarf, but otherwise dressed as a typical young American, she waited her turn and ordered a pastry. Behind the counter, a clerk responded with insults. Pegging her as Muslim, he denied her service, added demeaning comments, and demanded she leave. In front of other customers, she protested and asked several what she should do, and if they would help. Meanwhile the clerk continued his insults.

The other customers could not have known, but the young woman and the clerk were actors. They staged the insulting situation to see what others in the bakery would do when faced with blatant prejudice. A clear case of insulting behavior based on appearance and the image cast by it was created; how would onlookers respond?

ABC's situation tapped several important American realities. First, the image of a young woman in a head scarf now has powerful social import. Though her attire was otherwise unexceptional, and her behavior was entirely appropriate, she was flagged as someone representing a threat to American life. Muslims have become the embodiment of people who are different. They have also become emblematic of the threat of difference to American life, a sense many Americans share. The ABC News experiment was telling. How would onlookers in the bakery respond? What would they do?

Thus the second reality this episode tested was the readiness of Americans to step into a situation of social conflict involving people they did not know. In what sense do we see one another as neighbors, especially if the neighbor is Muslim? Perhaps the results of this experiment should not be given too much weight. This was one bakery in one community on one morning. Repeated many times in varied settings, there may have been more telling, nuanced results. Nevertheless the responses were notable.

A few people joined the insults, or simply endorsed the clerk's behavior. When approached by an ABC commentator, they defended the clerk and their support for him. A few other customers defended the young woman, some assertively. Several promptly left, loudly declaring they would never do business in that bakery again. One man confronted the clerk and in charged, emotional terms defended the young woman and her religion. But most people did nothing. A few slid quietly away, while others simply stood silently by, hearing the insults and watching the confrontation that resulted.

Generalizations are risky on such a small sample. But the responses in that bakery suggest wider American currents. There is considerable prejudice against Muslims, and there has been considerable prejudice against others in the American past. There is also a long American tradition of fair play and even hospitality to strangers. Finally there also is an American impulse to keep out of what is perceived to be other people's business, and to avoid stepping into controversy. Just as congregations steer clear of religious and cultural difference, individual Americans, even people of faith, appear to have ready recourse to privacy. A majority of Americans prefer to avoid stepping forward in charged situations.

The net result in this bakery is that a few were blatantly prejudiced, and a few spoke up. But most people did nothing. It is tempting to cheer the persons who rushed to defend the young woman. Yet a troubling question remains: why was the majority silent? Could they have been empowered in some way not merely to rally around a victim of prejudice? Could they have been motivated and equipped to work to reduce prejudice based upon a person's appearance and false associations linked to it? What lessons can be drawn? How could future situations like this be handled better?

In a nutshell the Texas bakery captures America's challenge as religious pluralism increases. Islam is a prime example of the new American pluralism. Islam casts images that trigger vehement, extensive prejudice. More alarming, prejudice against Muslims taps a deeper polarization and alienation in American life. Worse still, many Americans seem powerless to address such conflict and remain silent. No doubt a large number of Americans who remain silent are themselves religious. But they allow fear and even hostility to fester.

ABC News took no religious census of the people in the bakery. There were no hints of who may have been Christian or Jewish among the customers, or who may have been active in a congregation nearby. But it would seem likely that active members of congregations were among the people in the bakery when the clerk began to insult a young woman in a head scarf. Should we assume that members of congregations will act in the same way as other bakery customers? That some would be prejudiced; some would dare to confront prejudice; and many would be silent. But what should a person who is Christian or Jewish do in such a situation?

Shouldn't faithful people be proactive in standing with other people of faith in the face of prejudice? In part the goal of this workbook is to encourage a different and better response from the faithful people who make up America's congregations. I believe that members of American faith communities can be encouraged not only to respond to prejudice, but to address the deeper polarization that has infected our public life. Even more, local faith communities can be equipped to find and engage the common good of their communities in the midst of the new religious difference. Difference does not eliminate a substantial basis for common concerns, common affirmations, and common initiatives.

THE POWER OF IMAGES

It can surface in the most casual circumstances. As four women casually played cards, they discussed the morning headlines, much as they do every time they meet. Several groaned about the latest reports of wars and conflicts then resumed studying their hands. But one woman unexpectedly erupted: "You know they want to kill us all." Puzzled, another woman asked: "What do you mean?" "Those Muslims," she sputtered in response. Then she added, "Don't you realize they're taught to kill us? You might think they're your friends. But they are waiting for the right moment to strike us again."

The association of Islam with a variety of terrorist attacks and threats of attacks, and with upheaval in the Middle East and Asia, is a deep conviction for many. To be sure, terrorist networks such as Al Qaeda, and several radical movements such as the Taliban in Afghanistan, proclaim Islam as their basis and their motivation. But they represent a tiny percentage of the Muslim world, and their association with major trends and events is distant if such a connection exists at all. Nevertheless the link between Islam and extremism is consistent for many, including some national leaders. As chair of the House Committee on Homeland Security, Representative Peter King said that over 80 percent of Muslims in America are radicalized.[1] The source for such a statistic has not been named. But the force of images from the media and from public figures such as King has not been lost on the public. More reliable statistics tell how extensive religious prejudice has become as American religious pluralism expands.

Early in 2010 the Gallup organization released a study of what it termed "Religious Perceptions in America." The survey looked at attitudes toward four religions: Buddhism, Christianity, Islam, and Judaism. The findings were sobering. Nearly half of the respondents (43 percent) admitted to holding prejudice against Muslims. Worse, those holding prejudice also claimed to know something about the religion and even to personally know a Muslim. The tendency to be prejudiced runs deep for Americans. So deep that prejudice against Muslims showed a high correlation with prejudice against Jews. Even presumed familiarity with a people and their faith did not mitigate suspicion.

At about the same time, Lifeway Research, the research arm of the Southern Baptist Convention, released a study of attitudes of Protestant clergy. If anything, the clergy proved to be more prejudiced. Half of the clergy believe Islam is evil, and over half think Muslims are dangerous. The basis for holding these attitudes was unclear, given the dimensions of the study. But the findings suggest feelings that are deeply felt and not easily swayed.

These statistics are testimony to the power of negative images. Worse, this data suggests that people of faith are complicit in the stereotypes and prejudice that surround Islam. This is not to say that Islam does not have issues with extremism in its midst, as most Muslims readily admit. But this is to say that all religions have problems with extremism and that the percentage of militant Muslims, as we shall see, is tiny. The overwhelming majority of Muslims are being unfairly tagged and treated in ways that hardly reflect the faith Christians, Jews, and people of other religions claim to embody.

Images evoke prejudice. Images that are common in Islamic contexts, notably forms of dress, are firmly linked to fears of terrorism for the majority of non-Muslims in America. This is an alarming reality. It not only confirms the power of images, it reflects an inability of faithful people and congregations to combat prejudice. The power of such negative images also undercuts any possibility for identifying points of agreement and launching collaborations that would address issues in the communities where they live alongside one another.

But worst of all, when people of faith and their faith communities allow such distorted images to go unchallenged, they are failing to live up to the basic tenets of their own faith. Love of God and love of neighbor are core principles of the three Abrahamic faiths. On such a basis one can be true to one's own tradition and able to build common initiative with people of a different faith.

It must be emphasized that this challenge is not limited to images and treatment of Muslims by non-Muslims. Muslims in America today have become emblematic of the growth of religious minorities and the new diversity of American religious and cultural pluralism. The problems associated with being Muslim in America also surface in the experience of people of other faiths. Writ large, the challenge all of religious America faces is the challenge of becoming American together. How can we hold different faiths, and different cultural and faith practices, and yet come together as Americans?

THE CHALLENGE OF BECOMING AMERICAN TOGETHER

It's Not the First Time

Sadly this is not the first time in U.S. history that prejudice has unfairly tagged one or another people because of their religious faith. Near the middle of the nineteenth century, fears of Roman Catholicism boiled over on occasion into violence and lingered for decades as outright prejudice. Large numbers of Irish immigrants, most fleeing a famine and seeking opportunity, triggered fears of a conspiracy by a foreign power that was determined to seize control of American life. The sight of nuns and priests in religious garb fueled suspicions of plots and sabotage. The result was incidents where mobs assaulted Catholics and Catholic facilities. In 1834, for example, a mob burned a convent in Charlestown, Massachusetts. In 1844, a series of riots in Philadelphia destroyed Catholic facilities there. Meanwhile the "Know-Nothing" movement gained political clout based on fears of immigrants, especially Roman Catholics.[2]

Even after violence and the Know-Nothing movement subsided, prejudice against Catholics lingered for a century. The election of John F. Kennedy as president in 1960 was seen as a milestone. For the first time a Catholic had been elected to the nation's highest office. Images cast by the Catholic Church that once had inadvertently fueled prejudice had become part of the American fabric and no longer provoked anger and violence.

Other images linked to prejudice against peoples and religions have proven more difficult to eradicate. Judaism has long been the recipient of prejudice, even after creation of the state of Israel and broad American support for it. Between 1979 and 1989 nearly ten thousand hate crimes against Jews were recorded by the Anti-Defamation League, including assaults, vandalism, and destruction of property. Although they represent a variety of cultural and national backgrounds, as do Muslims and Catholics and other religious groups, Jews in many American communities have been seen as a monolith and barred from educational and cultural opportunities. It is ironic that despite high levels of American public support for the state of Israel, prejudice against Jews in the United States has also remained high. Fortunately such prejudice has never reached European levels and has receded in recent years, partly from changes in public attitude and partly from recourse to laws that prohibit discrimination based on race or religion.

Actual conflict is a powerful stimulus of prejudice. Before September 11, 2001, likely the most cited date in American history was December 7, 1941, the day then–President Franklin Roosevelt said would "live in infamy." On that day Japanese aircraft launched from carriers conducted an unprovoked attack on American military facilities at Pearl Harbor, Hawaii, and surrounding installations. Caught off guard, thousands of Americans died and the United States was plunged into World War II.

American news media of the time soon were filled with prejudicial references to Japanese people. More than their nation's aggressive military assault, the people themselves were vilified and became objects of hatred. As a result, Japanese Americans living especially on the West Coast were taken from their homes and detained in camps as, in effect, prisoners of war. Considered suspect because of their ancestry, they were presumed guilty of conspiring to attack America. Even today images of December 7 will recall stereotypes and prejudice that engulfed millions of people because of the actions of a few.

Likely the most pervasive and historic prejudice has been directed against African Americans. The very fact of slavery reflected the most entrenched, deep-seated prejudice. After a bloody civil war ended slavery, true freedom for African Americans took more than a century to realize. Blatant, widespread prejudice and discrimination were social realities for African Americans that seemed insurmountable until the civil rights movement of the second half of the twentieth century. Even in the twenty-first century, the eradication of social scars left by racial prejudice remains a major American project.

Images and the prejudice they can evoke are difficult to remove, especially when rooted in actual, violent conflict. The images linked to Islam, sadly, have followed the well-trod path of American suspicion. But memory is the basis of faith, and remembering fully and completely is the basis of healing and hope. The most basic memories of faithful people and faith communities center on core principles, such as love of God and love of neighbor. Ironically Islam, which has become so emblematic of the new religious pluralism, and such a source of prejudice, strongly embraces these principles.

Yet Islam has received intense scrutiny and criticism. This is because Islam embodies a change in American society toward a new demographic profile, and this change elicits fear and prejudice in many Americans. In part, Islam has become emblematic because it is highly visible in certain respects: media coverage of Islam has conveyed images of people at prayer and women wearing head scarves if not full covering. But in this respect Islam is not alone; it also represents the new public presence of religious pluralism. In other words, America is becoming both more pluralistic and, in a new way, public in its religious life.

In response, American congregations, and the faithful people who worship in them, must shun prejudice and fear. Instead, congregations must show public leadership in their communities by reemphasizing the basic principles of their faith as a basis for taking fresh initiative. On the basis of faith principles that should be clear and readily understood, it may be possible to take steps toward collaboration amid difference. This task has become more urgent and yet more possible because of the new pluralism, as I shall explain.

American Values, Plural Faiths

When one looks beyond the prejudicial images and casual but ill-informed assumptions that fuel them, a startling realization surfaces: although most of America's expanding religious groups value their faith and order their lives by its precepts, they also are intent on living fully as Americans. They do not want to be known simply by their faith or their cultural heritages, as vital as these are for them. They are certain they can be the latest generation of people who are both faithful and American.

One anecdote illustrates how Islam and other forms of the new religious pluralism are seeking fresh public presence. In a suburban home of a medium-size American city, a middle-class family wakes up to begin a new day. The parents are professionals, one a teacher and the other a medical technician. There are two adolescent children, a boy and a girl, both students at a nearby public high school. The morning is quiet, until the family gathers for breakfast. Then it becomes apparent that the daughter intends to wear a head scarf to school.

This family of South Asian background is proudly yet quietly Muslim. They are active in a nearby "Islamic center," the term many American Muslims choose rather than "mosque," perhaps trying to demystify their faith. But their lives otherwise could be linked to any number of religious identities, or to none at all. They live as most Americans live. Then one morning, the youngest family member decides she will publicly declare that she is Muslim.

It was a few years after September 11, 2001, and this family, like many Muslims in America, did not want public attention. Proud of their faith and of their Islamic center, they felt the building's presence, and the prayers and activities it offered, were enough visibility. There had been no threats to them or their center, and nearby churches and a synagogue had been friendly, although from a distance. Annual dinners at the center had drawn local civic and professional leaders. The dinners always included local politicians who made warm speeches quoting Thomas Jefferson and James Madison on religious liberty. Over and over it would be emphasized that Muslims, and most newer Americans, were loyal, loved God, and put their energies into their jobs and families. Gradually Muslim leaders felt they were building the respect and trust all religious people deserve. Knowing their loyalty was doubted by many, Muslims in America have worked to win a place in American life.

This was apparent at a fund-raising event for a new Muslim-sponsored school in Virginia. The dinner was held in the banquet room of a large hotel. Hundreds of guests attended, many of them local leaders of other faiths as well as local civic officials. The president of the new school's board gave a speech that stressed the importance of education both to Islam and to participation in American life. Thomas Jefferson and James Madison were warmly quoted, especially on the theme of freedom of religion. The role of the school in equipping future citizens was stressed.

But for many Muslims, participation in public life is a subject that also elicits a note of caution. Individually many American Muslims are reluctant to surface political opinions. It is better to participate in group life and to affirm basic, civic values in the company of respected leaders than to stand alone. Yet one morning the teenage daughter in one family decided she would do just that. She was devout and proud, and by her own initiative she would declare publicly who she was and what she believed.

Her parents were distraught. Their daughter's simple act tapped their deep fears and the limits of their trust. They were committed to being loyal Americans. They believed in American values and institutions. But would their daughter bring harm to herself? If not harm, would she invite prejudice even from teachers who might dislike Muslims and might not evaluate her academic work fairly? How could she know she would be treated with respect? What if she lost friends? What if she was ridiculed in public? Why did she need to wear a head scarf? Why not work hard and just be quiet?

She persisted. She trusted her friends and teachers. She knew her high school. She would be fine. And as she looked back on that day a few years later, she could smile and imagined her parents would smile at the memory as well. Her friends in the room had listened quietly as she described that first time she wore a head scarf in public. As she concluded, several others added their own experiences. They were members of a Muslim student group at a local college. Most of the young women in the group wore head scarves, and several of the young men wore "thobes," long, simple, one-piece garments emblematic of men's dress in the Arabian peninsula. None of the young women wore traditional Islamic women's garments; most wore jeans. But modesty was a consideration, and most had arms as well as legs covered.

But apart from references to religion, and a few bits of attire, their references and their slang were typical of American college students. It was clear that they were finding a way to be both American and Muslim.

In his travels around the United States, Akbar Ahmed repeatedly discovered similar dynamics among Muslims of all ages: an intense pursuit of ways to be both genuinely Muslim and genuinely American. Yet Ahmed found no one way, no single form of being Muslim and American. In his book, *Journey into America*, Ahmed describes the lives of dozens of Muslims, most of whom have the goal of being constructive parts of American life. Many, like a young woman in a head scarf, intend a more public expression of their faith. But where they live and where they pray say much about Islam's many varieties and about America's religious difference in general. There are considerable regional and local variations.

A scholar, author, and diplomat, Ahmed wants to emphasize both Islam's internal diversity and the inherent loyalty to America of its adherents. In his travels, he finds a few strident voices criticizing America much as conservative Christians and Jews do. But most see their faith as the basis of their own American religious journey. Their faith secures strong moral values, their sense of belonging to friends and social groups in their communities, and the families they nurture. For them faith is the foundation of life lived with goodness and even compassion. Yet what they mean by Islam, and exactly how faith blends with daily life, can vary from one local setting to another, or literally from one individual to another.

Religious pluralism in America today has taken this local turn in every faith tradition. If one asks what it means to be Catholic or Jewish, Pentecostal or one of the many varieties of historic Protestantism, clusters of images come to mind. Not only is America an unprecedented spectrum of religious identities, each includes its own set of variations. Being Muslim is no one thing, just as being Baptist or Presbyterian or Hindu or Buddhist is no one thing.

To further complicate matters, many Americans say they are on personal spiritual journeys, leaving behind the faith (or no faith) in which they were raised, adopting a new faith, or perhaps one new faith after another. The student president of one Muslim campus group was raised in a suburban home that was nominally Protestant. But in his freshman year he converted to Islam. His dress, demeanor, and speech seemingly are unchanged. But he has immersed himself in study outside the classroom and now appears at student and local interfaith groups as a Muslim.

His story has counterparts in every religious tradition and every congregation. People come and go on the basis of personal searches. At times the search intends no permanent destination; the journey itself matters more. A family once appeared in a Protestant church and quickly became prominent. The parents soon chaired committees and led them well. The children became valued church school and youth group members. For several years things went well. Then suddenly the family left the congregation. When contacted, they had no complaints and wished the congregation well. But as a family they decided it was time for something new. The journey had to continue. So they had affiliated with a different church of a different tradition in a different neighborhood.

Many Americans today intend to be different religiously, perhaps even repeatedly. There are conversions to and from and within all faiths, and Islam shares in this American dynamic.

HOW CHRISTIANS RESPOND

While the United States has steadily become more religiously pluralistic in the past ten years, a variety of responses from the nation's Christians can be identified. Of course, for much of American history religious pluralism has meant variations of Christian belief and organization, including Christian denominations of American origin. Such Christian variety is even more the case in the early twenty-first century. The range of church, noninstitutional church, and spiritual and parachurch groups is unprecedented. Meanwhile Christians must also respond to a dramatic increase in the range of non-Christian religions. America retains a clear Christian majority of nearly 80 percent, and over 90 percent of all Americans say they believe in God. But the range of other beliefs and associated practices and values has never been so varied.

Islam epitomizes the challenges and opportunities of pluralism. How Christians respond to Muslims suggests how Christians respond to religious differences generally. The responses of Christians follow one of four tendencies. As you review these categories, consider your own personal inclination, as well as that of your congregation. Then consider why you and your congregation respond as you do. If there are particular stories that hint at your response, discuss them and consider what they mean. In the future, how will you decide how to respond? What is the most appropriate way for you to address religious difference in your community?

1. Assertive Responses

In the face of religious difference some Christians assert their distinctiveness and, typically, their sense of superiority. The most obvious way in which this surfaces is an emphasis on conversion. Some Christians, notably of a conservative and evangelical sort, seek to overcome difference by eliminating it. Although this approach to religious difference may seem cynical, or even sinister, it typically reflects a heartfelt faith.

If you believe that eternal salvation of one's soul requires a decisive, conscious moment of personal commitment to Jesus Christ as your Lord and Savior, you will likely view people of different faiths, notably Muslims and Jews, but even other Christians, with an urgent compassion. Given life's vagaries, one could die at any moment. What if one died without professing a commitment to Christ? From this perspective the only outcome would be eternal damnation.

This stance is consistent with a single-minded focus on evangelism, and on specific outcomes of it. It is not the only kind of assertive response to difference. Some Christians do not attempt to proselytize others, but act toward them in ways that suggest a superior attitude. This may occur in the official stances of religious institutions that presume a certain kind of authority, or in local religious life, even in interfaith conversations which some may presume to define and direct, whether they do so consciously or not. Given the size of America's Christian majority, examples of assertive response are common and varied.

2. Passive Responses

At the same time, some branches of American Christianity have little or no contact with religious difference. One survey of a major Protestant denomination with millions of members revealed that less than 5 percent of its congregations had any contact with Jews or Muslims. While conservative theological schools may offer courses encouraging the goal of proselytism among Muslims and Jews, the historic mainstream seminaries offer few courses on Islam or on interfaith relations in general. Most graduates of these schools, who become local pastors, have no training in the realities of Islam or Judaism or other faiths and only vague appreciation of the shifts in American religious pluralism.

What accounts for this silence? In part it reflects liberal Christianity's rejection a generation or more ago of old notions of mission and evangelism, which their denominations once sponsored and which focused on converting non-Christian peoples. Explicitly and implicitly, the old evangelism, like current forms used by assertive Christians, declared cultural as well as religious superiority. But large numbers of Western missionaries came home, and those who remained focused their work on creating indigenous church structures and leadership.

But the pendulum swung too far. The missionaries not only left prematurely in most cases, before indigenous church life had taken hold, but historic Protestant interest in other peoples and cultures faded. It seemed too aligned with abuses of Western influence and with a coercive presentation of Christianity. Liberal Christians withdrew in the name of honoring religious and cultural difference. But withdrawal meant knowledge and involvement with peoples of other faiths faded, with nothing to replace it.

Over the past generation liberal Protestantism also faced a series of crises at home. Well-publicized conflicts over human sexuality, belief, leadership and the direction of church life, and securing financial support amid economic strain have challenged institutional structures and assumptions. As a result, denominational and judicatory structures are largely focused inward. Amid weakened infrastructures, congregations must secure their own resources and find their own way. In these circumstances talk of Muslims, interfaith relations, and religious pluralism seem like luxuries that cannot be afforded, however important they may be.

3. Complicit Responses

The reality of religious difference is not lost on all mainstream church leaders or on liberal Protestantism in particular. One scholar, Paul Knitter of Union Theological Seminary in New York, has written a daring book that has prompted important conversations. In *Without Buddha I Could Not Be a Christian*, he reflects on his years as a Roman Catholic missionary, on his long academic career, and on his wife's faith as a Buddhist. How could he reconcile these distinct influences? Knitter seeks a synthesis of them. Carefully he probes both key Christian and Buddhist beliefs and perspectives, and concludes that they inform one another. He constructs a way to, in his mind, be both Christian and Buddhist. It makes impressive reading and admirable sentiment. But can this work practically guide other people in different situations?

In any city with an interfaith group, or simply among people of goodwill, one will find something similar. Sooner or later, someone will say: "Well, after all, we all believe pretty much the same thing. We just come at it differently." The intention is kind and to be welcomed at a time when there is far too much hostility between faiths. But such sentiment hardly does justice to Knitter, or to the reality of religious difference.

If Muslims, Jews, and Christians are to honor one another, they must not be superficial or erroneous about similarities and differences. Honoring one another means living together in the midst of difference. Understanding difference, stripping it of myths and prejudices, and finding genuine similarities are the tasks. We all are human and people of God. But how our humanity and our faith shape our lives have important variations. We must learn to be clear about our own religious identities without diminishing others. In other words, we must learn to be people of particular faiths in a world of plural faiths.

4. Cooperative Responses

Since September 11, 2001, there have been hopeful signs at the grassroots of American life. In many cities interfaith groups have arisen, a few offering significant, ongoing programs. The Tanenbaum Center in New York City, for instance, has developed seminars and programs designed to promote understanding among civic and business groups. Its focus should be emulated widely as it seeks to instill understanding into daily life.

The Tri-Faith Initiative in Omaha, Nebraska, has launched an unparalleled example of cooperation for urban development. Jewish, Muslim, and Christian leaders have joined forces to build adjacent worship spaces and a fourth, shared multifaith center. These structures will anchor a complex of retail, housing, and medical facilities that will cost over two hundred million dollars. Metropolitan Omaha has nearly a million people, but such a project would have a major impact on communities of any size.

The Omaha initiative readily received approval from city authorities, and widespread goodwill from the community, but such is not always the case. The so-called "mosque at ground zero" controversy in New York has shocked leaders of all three faiths. Deep sensitivities were touched by a proposal to create a shared facility under Muslim initiative several blocks from the World Trade Center site. Clearing the air, addressing misperceptions, and launching a fresh initiative have proven difficult given the extent of publicity and suspicion. But addressing fears and building common response to common challenges is the best way forward.

There is a legacy of cooperation for social good that unites people of different faiths. For generations different faith groups have worked together to feed hungry persons, house the homeless, and offer job training and placement. People of different faiths work together in counseling centers and hospitals. They give equal emphasis to their personal religious identities and to the broad religious missions of their organizations. Religious groups have long operated facilities that welcome all faiths. It is clear that American education and philanthropy have religious roots and continue to be defined by religious intention, specifically compassion for human need.

At a time of increasing social need and new religious pluralism, the call for interfaith cooperation is as great as ever. Not only does the nation benefit, interfaith understanding rises. Such initiatives must arise from local initiative, often the work of individual congregations. The weakening of religious institutions, combined with fresh spiritual energies and pluralism, means that congregations are at the forefront. They can encourage and equip local leadership for interfaith cooperation in a way that challenges suspicion and enhances life in your community.

QUESTIONS FOR DISCUSSION

1. Think of the last time that something happened and you felt you should speak up, but you did not. What held you back? What would help you to speak up in the next situation?
2. What American social values readily resonate with your faith? What values are in conflict with what you believe as a person of faith?
3. What stance has the congregation you know best taken toward the reality of difference in your community?

INDIVIDUAL AND GROUP EXERCISES

1. Research suggests that in bullying situations, if just one person speaks up, then bullying is more likely to stop. Do you agree or disagree? Why?
2. What do you think makes us focus on the minor differences between groups of people rather than the major similarities between them? As human beings, are we more alike than we are different?
3. This book says that "all religions have problems with extremism." Can you cite any personal experience with religious extremism? What do you think gives rise to such extremism, when faith encourages "love"?
4. America has been considered the melting pot for diverse groups of people; the ideal was that people would "assimilate" into American life. What do you think of the image of the melting pot now? Is a different metaphor better? How about the metaphor of a quilt?
5. Given the four approaches of congregations to difference described in this chapter, what have you seen and what are you most comfortable with?

LEARNING FROM OTHER FAITHS

In the past, different faith groups have used different approaches to deal with the conflicts that come with diversity. However, more recently, each faith group has liberal, conservative, and extremist factions within it. Select three faith groups and Google them to determine how difference is handled in different parts of each faith.

SCRIPTURE LESSON

"Do not be conformed to this world, but be transformed by the renewing of your minds, so that you may discern what is the will of God—what is good and acceptable and perfect. For by the grace given to me I say to everyone among you not to think of yourself more highly than you ought to think, but to think with sober judgment, each according to the measure of faith that God has assigned. For as in one body we have many members, and not all the members have the same function, so we, who are many, are one body in Christ, and individually we are members one of another." (Romans 12:2–5)

What does this scripture suggest in terms of handling differences?

> "For everything there is a season, and a time for every matter under heaven . . . a time to keep silence, and a time to speak." (Ecclesiastes 3:1, 7)

In dealing with conflict, how do you know when to speak and when to keep silent?

PRAY

"In the face of religious difference some Christians assert their distinctiveness and, typically, their sense of superiority."

Pray for the ability to treasure your faith and share it with others in ways that are not prideful.

Pray for the courage to speak up against bigotry.

5

THE CHALLENGE CONGREGATIONS MUST FACE

WHERE DO YOU STAND?

Where does your congregation stand in its encounter with difference? What has worked or not worked in your experience? Do you avoid or combat or gloss over differences? Has understanding developed, and could cooperation follow? The categories listed in the previous chapter may not be satisfying to you. You will find shades of gray in your life and the life of your congregation. The categories may not adequately reflect the nuance you experience. As you consider how you and your congregation respond to the reality of difference in your midst, a basic fact surely proves striking: the encounter with difference forces you to be clear about who you are, what you believe, and how you act on the basis of your beliefs. In the face of difference you cannot assume to know, you must be clear. This is a challenge that congregations must face because of the reality of difference.

This is not simply the case if you encounter Muslims in your community. Islam has become emblematic of the challenge of facing difference in the wider world. Islam embodies religious and cultural complexities that are both visible and difficult to sort out. Islam has become embedded in major global events in ways that compel Americans to reconsider the rest of the world and our role in it. Islam also represents the shifting demographic profile of the United States and the changing face of local American life. Above all, Islam is a major world religion with a similar heritage.

But Islam in this respect is simply a vivid example of much larger trends. Difference is the unavoidable reality for most American communities and for the congregations in them. Towns and neighborhoods that seemed well defined are shifting in their populations. At the same time historic religious institutions face tensions over belief and practice as well as economic strains. In many cases judicatories and national denominational headquarters have faced program and staff cuts, a trend that shows no promise of abating. The result is something of a perfect storm for congregations: financial, doctrinal, program, and leadership directions are uncertain.

With some justification, many leaders of congregations say they cannot afford to deal with religious and cultural difference, in their vicinity or beyond. Perhaps they face difficult internal issues and even conflict over their leadership and direction. To worsen the situation many congregations face the challenge of inadequate or deteriorating buildings and facilities. Aging physical plants make facing other challenges seem secondary. The changing demographic face of one's community seems like an academic discussion for which there is little time. Religious and cultural difference nearby may give you pause, but surely it can wait. There is enough to do in your home before you venture outside.

So it may never occur to you that the presence of difference of all sorts offers you and your congregation the best possible resource. The remainder of this book is written in this vein. How you respond to difference, as the last chapter's categories suggested, should awaken consideration of who you are, what you believe, and how you act on the basis of your beliefs. There is no adequate response to the internal challenges of the congregation without clarity on these questions.

As you consider your congregation's needs and its faith profile, a basic reality becomes apparent: there is no wall of separation between your congregation and the wider world. The people who enter your building, sit in your pews and chairs, mingle at receptions, attend classes, and join committees bring the world and its realities through the doors. You can try to overlook or to decry "the world," but inevitably you must respond to it. The encounter with difference is unavoidable. In the face of difference you must be clear about who you are, as a person of faith and as a faith community. This clarity is the first step toward addressing the issues you assumed were simply internal to the congregation. Finding direction in a complex world is a primary reason why people seek congregations. Religious and cultural differences heighten the personal questions and issues many people face.

Even more, the emphasis on building understanding and cooperation with those persons who are different is precisely the path your congregation must walk to address its most pressing issues. For the sake of finding solutions, diverse perspectives must be heard and appreciated in your discussions. Hearing different points of view, like seeing the reality of difference in your local setting, can be difficult. Divergent viewpoints are not easily blended; doing so becomes a supreme test of leadership. Even seeing and hearing difference can surface powerful, negative reactions.

It is easy to feel that difference is a threat, that it portends loss. However legitimate their presence and genuine their hopes, people who are different from what you take to be the norm, inside and outside the congregation, can be seen as threats. When this thought appears, you and your congregation can falter and lose an opportunity to strengthen your life together.

Often the presence of difference of all sorts turns competitive. What fuels competition is a fear of impending loss. The world as we have known it seems to be eroding. Familiar landmarks that could evoke nostalgia are gone. People and tasks that once consumed us are no more. The people we now see in our midst can loom as rivals who have somehow "taken over." It becomes tempting to think that belief and values that were precious are in decline. The world that once was properly ordered seems to crumble. Of course not everyone believes the world once ran so perfectly. But in a congregation it becomes tempting to assume that once there was a necessary clarity, direction, and assurance. The fact of difference seems to shake those foundations. The world as it was must be defended lest all that has been precious is lost.

The fact of difference forces us to be clear about who we are, what we believe, and how we act as a result. For many people and their congregations the path to this clarity is clear: the fact of difference is bad and we must defend our faith and our way of life against intruders who would corrupt them. People of other faiths and cultures, perhaps wearing distinctive dress or speaking their native language, appear to be rivals. Increasingly this is a reality of the cities and towns where we live.

The temptation is to adopt what has been called "zero-sum" thinking. Drawn from abstract mathematical theory, zero sum in the realm of social relations means an inherent competition. If one individual or group appears to gain, then another must lose. The world seems to be a limited resource accessible to only an aggressive few; if some have access, others cannot. Like a cake with only so many slices, some accustomed to large portions will lose if new faces appear at the table. Thus an intense anger and fear of loss can dominate discussions of difference. Thus congregations try in vain to keep the world out.

An extreme instance of this impulse was discovered at a small, urban congregation. As the neighborhood changed, enough members with enough resources remained to keep it afloat. But as the numbers reduced, they resolved that they would only have one worship service a week, with an interim clergyperson, and that every member would have a key to the building. The few members of this congregation could literally afford to keep the world out.

Generally, when this impulse surfaces, the result is that people choose sides, excluding, avoiding, or vilifying those who are different. The imprint of zero-sum thinking can be seen vividly in American politics. Two political parties, representing opposing philosophies (perhaps not as opposed as they imagine), square off against one another. Each party is intent on defending precious values; each readily believes those values and the way of life they commend are threatened. The source of the threat lies in the distortions and ambitions of their opponents. But those opponents are blatantly wrong and their self-serving policies would wreak havoc if pursued. Discussion and certainly any consideration of the opponents' views risk a dangerous "compromise." Indeed "compromise" of one's views and intentions is almost as bad as the opponents themselves. The way forward entails rigid adherence to one's values and aggressive defense of them.

This standoff becomes a stalemate that frustrates practical solutions for pressing issues. Solution resembles compromise if it is not outright victory by one side or the other. Such a logjam has been apparent in national politics. It has also been clear in local life, in congregations as well as in civic life. This is the well-discussed "culture wars," a contest between liberals or progressives, and conservatives or traditionalists, as the contenders are variously known. Once more both sides depict themselves as the embodiment of truth broadly and religious as well as

American values specifically. Seeing the highest possible stakes, namely the survival of treasured ways of life, both sides have competed doggedly. They agree on only two things: there is a social, religious, and values crisis, and this is a win-lose competition.

Zero-sum thinking produces conspiracy theories, lawsuits, angry e-mails and blogs, and the denigration of those who differ. Religion is prone to such energies and susceptible to individuals who would heighten such tensions. This is because religion proclaims sacred principles, promotes faith community, and extols public virtues. Shifts in society can be construed as decline and blamed on difference. Difference can even be assigned evil motives and targeted as the enemy.

Because religion incorporates powerful strands of memory, the persistence of zero-sum thinking is enhanced. Memory is a powerful human experience that can surface innocently. In the midst of a demanding day a song on the car radio can transport you to another day and earlier circumstances. The music triggers memories of a moment you could savor forever. Particular people come to mind, and you smile as you think of them. Likely you were younger and living a life you would relish having again, at least as you recall it. It is easy to put on rose-tinted glasses and to recall a moment when life required no explanation. Everything made sense. Everyone understood. The world was as it should be. We treasure the memory as if it were the reality.

Was there such a moment, or even several moments, when life made sense, and you could flow easily among people and experiences? Was it a time of innocence and youth? Or, truly, was this a time when wonder and possibility took concrete form? Hopefully there was just such a time of innocence when you were young, and hopefully there have been genuine moments when life's meaning was clear and easily grasped. When a song distracts, there are memories that command instant attention. We think in similar ways of our congregations and their faith.

Yet we are all prone to nostalgia and even fantasy, as individuals and as congregations. Given a few grains of truth, memory can easily distort. It is likely that we were never as strong, clear, confident, or accomplished as we now recall. The people and relationships that captivate us were surely not as golden as memory now describes. There must have been some fault lines reflecting disagreement and rivalry. At times the people we now idolize were not as close or as flawless as we are prone to think. The group that now appears so tightly woven actually had a number of loose threads. The now glorious adventures really were mundane or barely happened at all. Life just was not as ideal as we now wish.

There is nothing wrong with nostalgia, if it is identified as such. When we treat our personal memories as something more than they were, there seems little harm. Nostalgia can be a wonderful, daydreaming distraction to otherwise ordinary moments. But nostalgia can substitute for memory in ways that introduce harmful distortions. It becomes tempting to believe that there was a time when a nation or a religion existed in pure form, as it properly should. The image of a pure moment becomes dangerous myth, and with it the more dangerous myth that some evil, external force has brought corruption and decline.

Extremists of all religious and political sorts use such a device: what was pure has been corrupted, and the stain of corruption must be removed for purity to be restored. It becomes tempting to blame an identifiable group for this plight. At various times, Catholics, Jews, Japanese and other Asian peoples, and African Americans have been blamed. Now Muslims seem to be the culprits. Somehow confronting them would pave the way for eliminating threat and recalling the nation to wholeness. Elsewhere such logic has given rise to horrific persecution; the targeting of Jews in Nazi Germany offers one of history's most gruesome examples. But many less blatant or murderous prejudices reveal the same assumption: purity of national life, or of belief, requires neutralizing those who are seen as offending parties.

Of course no such purity, or such a single-minded path to it or from it, can ever be found, if memory is used rightly. The very pursuit of purity will prove fruitless, and numerous people will be harmed in the process. Even congregations, and the local communities in which they sit, must beware of the lure of nostalgia. This is especially true when the idea that someone is to blame for evident decline takes hold. The mere sight of a woman in a head scarf can surface deep-seated anger with astonishing power to harm.

Fortunately memory is not always nostalgia, and nostalgia usually arises innocently. Other kinds of memories come to the surface less easily and bring no joy when they do. All of us carry the memories of hurt, loss, and disappointment. In some instances the hurt no longer controls us. A childhood injury, perhaps with painful cuts or even a broken bone, is recalled as painful and requiring a time of healing. But hurt from that experience exists only in memory and no longer in fact. Other memories, however, if we dare to recall them at all, have healed only incompletely, if at all. We are unlikely to seek them, but they surface with dreadful force, evoked by songs or sights or names, or by their own relentless power.

Such memories also are easily exaggerated. Only now, they are hardly sources of power and possibility. Instead they strip us of power, causing us to stall emotionally and spiritually. In varying ways the memory of September 11, 2001, has affected many Americans in this way. For many people, present and past, there have been times of painful, irreversible loss, which has been persistent and difficult to resolve. Just as we must acknowledge nostalgia for what it is, good and bad, we are not whole until we face painful memories honestly. Neither embellishing nor avoiding, we must face who we have been and what we have been through. Although it can be misleading, memory rightly used is the basis of reconciliation and hope.

REMEMBERING AND LEARNING

According to theologian Miroslav Volf, the goal of memory is not to remember as we are prone to do. Volf understands painful memory. As a student in communist Yugoslavia in the early 1980s he was drafted into the military, as were most young men. But he was an evangelical Christian, an advocate of nonviolence, and an opponent of Marxism. These convictions not only put him into the status of a social minority, they called attention to him. Military authorities soon judged him to be an enemy of the regime. The result was a lengthy period of detention and interrogation by military police, especially a figure he refers to simply as "Captain G."

The memory of interrogation has haunted Volf. But he tapped this memory to frame his notable book, The End of Memory.[1] In this book Volf asks a question, based on his own experience, that haunts everyone: how do we "remember rightly"? The question cannot be avoided because memory is inevitable. But it is also a pressing issue because the three Abrahamic faiths all are grounded in memory. Their most sacred convictions surround pivotal places, people, and events.

For Jews, for example, memory of the ancient journey to a promised land was followed by the rise of an ancient nation, of internal discord, the attack of a foreign power, and eventual captivity in a remote land. Later, there was return from exile and the rise once more of a nation with Jerusalem as its center, followed by the loss of the sacred land and dispersal, especially to Europe.

For Christians, sacred memory begins on a Jewish foundation. But Christian memory diverges with the appearance of Jesus, with his first followers, and with the organization of the church. Christian memory also shifts significantly to Europe, but then traces waves of expansion that would encompass the globe.

Similarly, Islam is rooted in memory, also centered on a pivotal figure. Like Christians, Muslims recall a powerful sense of possibility that gave rise to waves of expansion and the creation of a diverse people linked broadly by core beliefs and practices.

Debates about the role of faith center on what memories are central, how they should be recalled, and on the implications for living faithfully as individuals and as faith communities in the present.

Faith communities, especially at local levels, such as congregations, provide frameworks for remembering. In this way both personal joys and pains can be seen in fresh light, given sacred perspective, and hopefully resolved. Memories, by nature, are not forgotten; they have been called to mind. But they can be seen in a perspective that invites us to be whole, within ourselves and with others. For Volf this includes facing the reality of evil but driving out its dark realities and seeking the light of redemptive possibility even in its midst. We must remember, but we need not be controlled by, what happened in the past. We must ask how we are called to live in the present in light of memories of the past.

When the story of September 11, 2001, is recalled, for example, different aspects surface, some of which prove surprising. Of course the day was framed by hateful acts of destruction. But even when we consider these evil acts from various angles, we discover more. We recall the firemen, police, and other "first responders" who rushed in, some giving their lives. They were Christians, Jews, Muslims, and, indeed, people of all faiths or no faith. They were trained to face danger for the sake of giving aid. Memory recovers people who spontaneously went to nearby hospitals to donate blood and to offer assistance. In New York, scores of cafés and delis offered food and water to anyone walking by who needed it. Doors opened and strangers were welcomed with no questions asked. There was no hesitation because of race, religion, or politics. In a time of shared crisis, there was an instinct to pull together as Americans.

When tapped honestly and fully, memory unfolds hope and possibility. Even within painful memories, there can be a discovery of new paths, of ways out of what traps us, a promise of a new and better day. Far from confining us to what we have always been, memory, when used as a lens on the wider world, can free us. There is the potential for discovery of a new way, and perhaps even a fresh sense of wonder.

The memories of Muslims, Christians, and Jews include painful images of one another. Each faith bears painful images of harm inflicted on one by the others. For Muslims, the Crusades were a brutal invasion, even though Christians at the time defended it as rescuing the holy land. One of history's most systematic genocides, the Holocaust, is burned into memories of the twentieth century and continues to shape policies and events.

Over the centuries there have also been armies marching on one or another land in the name of one or another faith. The "fall" of the ancient city of Constantinople (now Istanbul) to a Muslim army became a searing loss in the eyes of Christian Europe. Less dramatic but more systematic, colonialism by European powers redefined lands where people of other faiths lived, juggling historic boundaries and creating nations to satisfy European policy designs. With colonialism has come economic and cultural imbalance, also serving as a source of resentment.

In recent decades there has been a spate of terrorist attacks. The rationale for them has been a striking back at memories of injustice and desecration. Thus memory lingers powerfully and triggers world-shaping events, often in the name of faith, but also linked to blurred economic and political and cultural circumstances. Without denying the reality of historic grievances and injustices, for which religion has often been used as justification, it is remarkable how memory has been used to accentuate the divisive aspects of difference, and to fuel zero-sum thinking.

However, there are alternative forms of memory that can counter the genuine legacy of insult and grievance. At various times, in a wide range of places, people of different faiths and cultures have lived beside one another successfully and happily. There have even been circumstances where Jews, Muslims, and Christians have lived together in harmony. The most cited of these is Cordoba, in southwest Spain. There, for over five hundred years, a large city and a remarkable culture arose. In a Muslim political framework people of the three Abrahamic faiths created historic creativity and prosperity. The face of one faith having political sway did not mean disenfranchisement for the other two faiths. All three worked together for the common good with remarkable results. Eventually, rivalry within and among the faiths coupled with economic decline to end this productive stability. After centuries of productivity, zero-sum thinking surfaced.

Cordoba has not been the only example of a common social fabric uniting people who seemingly would be in perpetual competition. In various places around the Mediterranean, understanding and cooperation have arisen when people have dared to pursue the common good. Even in historic Palestine, before the founding of the modern state of Israel, people of all three faiths have lived as neighbors and even as members of the same families. Whether actually related or not, formal and informal ties between the three faiths encouraged local cooperation. People of different faiths have not only lived nearby, they have created civic means of addressing common issues and celebrating their common life. There are fascinating examples of people of faith building civic spirit.

Beyond hurts and even evils perpetrated against one another with faith used to justify, there are deeper affirmations and promises when faith is rightly recalled. On a common footing, each faith in its own way calls for compassion and cooperation. Tapping memories of times when there was respect, when peoples lived together, and when cooperation seemed possible is crucial. Recovering shared affirmations and asking how we can affirm together become the basis of reconciliation. So also in congregations, where all espouse the same faith, there can be dramatic differences and painful memories. Recalling honestly, learning to speak to one another in fresh ways, and seeking basic faith affirmations can shine light on a new path. Memory rightly used awakens hope.

TOWARD HIGHER GROUND

A Morning Walk

The presence of difference compels us to be clear about who we are, what we believe, and how we act on the basis of our beliefs. Congregations bear memory in several forms. They carry the memories that are central to the sacred truths of their traditions. They also bear the memories of their people and the communities in which they are located. In some congregations there is ready confidence about what they believe and who they should be in their local setting.

Comfortable assumptions, however, may not stand up to examination. Memory of our faith's core principles and of our local community can become one-sided. A dread of difference can foster zero-sum thinking. Step-by-step we can overlook the fullness of memory in a mistaken defense of sacred principles that seem to be threatened. The possibility of understanding and cooperation to bridge our differences then fades. How do we move beyond suspicion and competition to a place where our individual faiths build common good? It has happened before in other places. How can it happen in the places where we live now?

One hot summer morning a small group of Jewish, Muslim, and Christian leaders in Richmond, Virginia, went in search of higher ground together. Specifically they climbed one of the city's original hills. Still a prominent spot, it affords a panoramic view of the downtown, of some of the oldest neighborhoods, and of local industry. On a clear day interstate highways can be seen teeming with cars, and distant suburbs beckon. The growth of the area is apparent. With that growth, religious and cultural differences have also become more evident. On this morning, the group symbolized the city's encounter with difference.

These religious leaders needed the broad view afforded them by higher ground. They could bring the city's dynamics into conversation with each of their faiths. But then they needed to step into the city's history so they could remember fully and begin to remember together. Soon, having come down from the hill, they were walking the Slave Trail, a planned path beside the James River into Richmond's old commercial center. As a guide explained, the Slave Trail follows paths along which enslaved human beings were led. Here people in chains were unloaded from ships to be bought and sold. There they were held as prisoners in grim conditions. Treated as property to benefit others, they were trapped in an inhuman institution that contradicted American ideals of freedom and justice.

From atop a hill these religious leaders could have stayed with a broad overview, and talked in warm general principles. Walking where shackled people once walked, they were forced to apply their ideals of faith to specific realities. They had to remember the past fully and tell its story honestly. As they walked and grappled with had happened there, a noticeable change began: by working together on the legacy of their city, they built rapport. No longer simply Muslims, Jews, and Christians, they were people of faith concerned for the place where they live. Telling the full story of the community gave them a basis for common purpose.

There can be no common purpose without a common story. This is true within our congregations, and it is true in the communities where we live. People of faith are called to be alert to the power of the past and to develop the means of linking local experience to larger, historic fact and to sacred principles. Each faith tradition sees God at work in the course of human experience. Each tradition also sees human fallibility and offers pathways to redemption. Careful retelling of the past together allows for common purpose to emerge. Simply meeting, walking, recalling, speaking, and listening become the building blocks. Difference is not erased. But difference brings a wealth of faith resources and offers broad, common ground.

The group was silent as its walk concluded. The encounter with painful memory had its intended impact. But over lunch there was a newfound freedom to speak openly about faith and local life. Trust was built, and it became possible to see that similar trends are shaping each of their faiths and each congregation these leaders represented. As they reflected on how to work together on the needs of their city, references to these trends readily surfaced, and they found they were speaking the same language. All American congregations, and the larger faith traditions they represent, face one or another aspect of the same set of trends.

A Basis for Cooperation

In using Islam as a key instance of difference, I have noted key trends among Muslims: youth, women, spirituality, education, and reform. These trends have counterparts in other religions and cultures, especially among Jews and Christians. For example, each religion is in the midst of energetic discussion of young people. For each, such discussions build upon long legacies of changes from one generation to the next. The older generation worries that the younger one will not learn the faith properly or at all. Special programs including classes, conferences, retreats, camps, and ceremonies of recognition are the result. Every religion also emphasizes the role of the family in raising children lovingly while instilling desired religious beliefs and moral values.

Similarly education is an historic emphasis for Jews and Christians as well as for Muslims. The examples of schools, colleges, and graduate schools founded and sustained under religious auspices are countless. Obviously education is crucial for conveying the faith. But education has also meant research and specialized training that draws on the tenets of faith. A deep compatibility between belief and learning is apparent in the Abrahamic religions.

In recent years, reform movements in many faiths have sought to educate in innovative ways. For example, some educational institutions affiliated with religious groups now offer online courses. Courses and events have spilled beyond the historic channels of religious institutions. A vibrant, diverse religious marketplace features education as its cornerstone.

Similarly the roles of women in many branches of Christianity and Judaism have shifted in recent decades. The most obvious change has been the ordination of women as clergy in some branches of these religions. In some instances, theological seminaries enroll equal numbers of women and men. Women have attained the highest leadership roles in some denominations and are accorded leadership authority as readily as men at all levels of religious life. If not fully realized in all branches of Judaism and Christianity, equality of opportunity for women has become a reality for many.

Movements of increased spirituality and religious observance stamp Jewish and Christian life as fully as they do the Muslim world. The array of such groups is so broad that an entire text could be devoted to it.

Every Jewish and Christian congregation has felt the influence of spiritually enlivened people and perhaps been challenged decisively by them. Broad searches for more profound faith, for deeper religious insight, and for more authentic lives are apparent.

It is ironic that many non-Muslims openly speak with fear of the influence of fundamentalism in Islam. The term "fundamentalism" arose in the early twentieth century in the United States as a small group of Protestant Christian leaders sought to place basic belief on a more dogmatic basis. Fundamentalism has become a certain kind of religious reform that has analogies across the Abrahamic faiths. It has tried to ground truth in religious law and to demand obedience as the measure of true belief. But if fundamentalism has counterparts in all religions, so do other, broader spiritual movements. These center less on notions of religious law and more on study, prayer, and service to people in need. And this spirituality has fueled movements of social reform.

Among the other Abrahamic faiths the most debated reality today would likely be the founding of the state of Israel in the wake of World War II. Nazi efforts at genocide of the Jewish people in Europe combined with long-standing dreams of a restored Jewish homeland to prompt mass emigration and the founding of a new nation. Disputed versions of how Israel was founded, what borders it has assumed, and how it acts in the name of national security are the sources of current conflict. Many American Christians rally to Israel's defense uncritically while others seek to resolve conflicts between Israel and its religious and political neighbors in ways that are acceptable to all.

Muslims see one of their holiest shrines, the Dome of the Rock at the Al Aqsa mosque in Jerusalem, at the center of the conflict. Muslims also see that a largely Islamic population, the Palestinians, have been disadvantaged. The lines of conflict based on divergent perceptions are extreme. The problem of difference in the Holy Land is acute. The repercussions across American religious life are genuine. It is possible that American religious leaders can speak with a freedom and a mutual concern that is more difficult elsewhere. Yet it is widely the case that holy places, including congregations and their buildings, become the source of conflict when they are situated in the midst of religious and cultural variety. Appreciation of the way in which a place becomes holy for the people of a particular faith is a major step toward reducing conflict and encouraging understanding.

Fortunately, all three faiths have experienced recent reform impulses. Reform along religious lines is an historic theme in American life that has drawn fresh energies in recent years. Of course, the "culture wars" that flared in the late twentieth century embody the ideals of religious conservatives and liberals for American life. Sensing moral decline, conservatives have pursued policies designed to strengthen moral life and boost the family while affirming a free market economy. Liberals adhere to an historic focus on social justice that would enlist government in expanding opportunities for minority groups. Curiously, Americans both emphasize the separation of church and state and presume that the nation needs the moral influence religion alone can provide. But there are long-standing debates about the proper ends and means of religion's social role.

The three Abrahamic faiths—Christianity, Islam, and Judaism—share similar challenges and similar trends. How we interpret them and address them differ according to our beliefs and our local settings. But understanding what we face in ways that respect differences while discovering similarities is the key to building understanding and cooperation. Interestingly neuroscientist and author Robert Wright anticipates such a future. Going beyond the bounds of science in his book *Nonzero*, Wright predicts that globalization will compel cooperation. Human cultures and even nature itself will seek paths to cooperation rather than competition. Zero-sum thinking arose as a primitive survival instinct but has outlived its original usefulness. Human development has reached a critical stage. Competition has become a recipe for failure. Far from protecting an imagined, threatened purity of sacred precepts and community, hostility to those who are different has become an historical dead end. Instead the challenge is to replace competition with cooperation.

Despite the reality of conflicts across every society and religion, Wright is optimistic. He perceives all of history and nature moving toward a great, cosmic fulfillment. He attaches inevitability to it, and suggests that forms of human experience that resist will falter. To the discomfort of some readers who seek only scientific ground, Wright even poses an image of God as the completion, if not exactly the creator. But while abstract consideration of his conclusions continues, one point is clear: the future of human experience must focus on cooperation. This is especially the case because religions and cultures that once existed in isolation now are face-to-face. They are encountering one another not only in a few places; the awareness of difference is a staple of daily life, in the media and in person.

For people of faith, such encounters compel clarity about who they are, with a focus on abandoning zero-sum thinking and acting. The feasibility of this large step has been tested in "A Common Word," as we discussed in chapter 3. In light of "A Common Word," the task of addressing difference in congregations and among people of faith has become clear: it centers on affirming the similarities and appreciating the true differences between people of the same and of varied faith traditions. There can be no barrier separating life in a congregation from the dynamics of its context. The variety of religious, cultural, and social perspectives of the area where a congregation is located must be seen as a resource.

One must not assume that difference represents an assault on one's views or feel that to get along one must somehow dilute one's views to accommodate other views. The intention must be to honor all persons and their views, presuming that each person stands on honorable ground. A process of finding intersections rather than building barriers can awaken the prospect of cooperation and reduce the specter of discord.

But what can this mean in practice? It is one thing to speak of loving God and one's neighbor in the abstract; such affirmations flow easily from the lips of faithful people. But, in the face of difference in local contexts, how can cooperation replace competition? In congregations, how can tensions over identity, direction, and leadership be resolved? Among the various faith communities of a city or town, what can be done to break down suspicion and forge common purpose? How can religion be more of a broad bond, spanning difference for the good of all? In the next chapter we begin to address these questions.

QUESTIONS FOR DISCUSSION

1. In your experience, have congregations been too absorbed in internal issues to give serious attention to issues in their local

community? If so, what sorts of internal issues have created this preoccupation?
2. Give an example of zero-sum thinking in your experience, in a congregation or in another setting such as work. How did this outlook take hold and with what results?
3. What makes a place holy? What places are holy to you? Why?

INDIVIDUAL AND GROUP EXERCISES

1. Identify two or three areas of conflict in your congregation. How did they arise? How have they been addressed, or avoided?
2. What are the needs of your congregation, and why are they priorities?
3. Is the presence of difference unavoidable? Do you agree or disagree? How does difference offer your congregation a resource?
4. Give some examples of zero-sum thinking in your congregation. This means a dynamic in which people believe they either win or lose. How have you seen such a cycle broken and people pull together?
5. Since God made us all, and yet we are different in varied ways, might God have revealed divine truth to different peoples in different ways?

LEARNING FROM OTHER FAITHS

What does it mean to love your neighbor? Research this question in the Bible, the Torah, and the Qur'an. Research it in secondary sources as well. Look at Paul Tillich's *The Shaking of the Foundation*, Prince Ghazi's *Love in the Quran*, and Jonathan Sacks's *The Dignity of Difference.*

SCRIPTURE LESSON

"'Teacher, which commandment in the law is the greatest?' He said to him, 'You shall love the Lord your God with all your heart, and with all your soul, and with all your mind.' This is the greatest and first commandment. And a second is like it: 'You shall love your neighbor as yourself.' On these two commandments hang all the law and the prophets.'" (Matthew 22: 38–40)

Who is your neighbor?

PRAY

The task of promoting interfaith understanding and cooperation centers on affirming the similarities, appreciating the differences, and building respect in the process. The challenge is to stand on one's own ground and to grasp that others must stand on theirs. Pray for understanding of this message in your daily life.

6

WHEN FASCINATION REPLACES FEAR

THE POSSIBILITY OF "THE OTHER"

In recent years many American Christians have been energized by the thought of an "emergent church." Every few centuries, perhaps even at regular intervals, institutionalized Christian hierarchies have been challenged by grassroots spiritual movements. Inevitably misrepresented by authoritarian structures, the deep truths of Christian faith and community have surfaced in unexpected ways in various local sites at the same time, followers of "emergence Christianity" typically hold. New forms of social experience, varied but spontaneous and true to Christianity's core principles, have gained traction. The result has been an historic series of movements to recapture the faith, a precedent that is being repeated now. Institutional religious structures and their inflexible ways must adapt or be swept aside. Periods of major Christian change, such as the Protestant Reformation of the sixteenth century in Europe, attest to the irresistible power of such moments.

As compelling as the idea of emergence Christianity has become, ironically it reflects narrow thinking. Rarely do followers of emergence acknowledge that the energies reshaping Christianity in North America today have counterparts in every religion, historically and in the present. Judaism and Islam have long histories of movements in pursuit of more authentic faith and life. In some measure the impulse has led to fundamentalist resistance to modern social trends and seeming religious accommodation. But even more, novel forms of spirituality have emerged to shape personal life and inspire faith community.

Spirituality has arisen in multiple forms, often with powerful influence. For example, many congregations of all faiths can attest to the power of the "charismatic" movement of the late twentieth century. Charismatic Christians claim to recapture the power of the day of Pentecost that energized the early church. Though at times divisive in congregations, the charismatic movement left a legacy of profound new depth of faith commitment for many people. It represented an emphasis on the immediate activity of God's spirit bringing healing, direction, and possibility. Greater clarity about one's faith as a way of life emerged. Greater attentiveness to the pursuit of shared expression became apparent. More deeply, more clearly, faith was no longer one membership among several for more people. Faith was a living, dynamic identity to which individuals and congregations gave energetic witness.

For some people and congregations the embrace of the charismatic movement and then of the emergent church has resulted in a great, inward turn. These spiritual energies have fostered intense effort to remake one's personal and family life. Fresh spiritual impetus has also been apparent in congregations, with prayer and study groups, retreats, and innovative liturgies typically resulting. The theme of "authenticity" pervades these intentions. By whatever name it is called—spirituality, renewal, or emergence—a broad pursuit of authentic faith and community has surfaced. "There must be something more," people find themselves thinking. Avidly they are pursuing and grasping it.

In part many people are reaching for "nonzero" circumstances. By large majorities Americans seem exhausted by conflict and division in public as well as religious life. They are also weary of ineffectual institutions of all sorts. Nor are they prepared to offer obedience to the dictates of institutional authorities. But rejection of tension and outmoded institutional modes is only part of the public mind. If people are tired of division they are energized by possibilities they sense in today's spiritual currents. This possibility focuses on building faith and community anew by their own efforts in their own circumstances. The "hands-on" approach is a hallmark of twenty-first-century spirituality. Local initiative to deepen one's faith and to have tangible impact because of it is pervasive. In many places, including perhaps your own setting, a fascinating conversation is taking shape.

In a new way people see themselves on a multidimensional journey. They are seeking a deeper, more authentic personal faith while exploring fresh forms of shared discovery within and beyond several faith sources at once. Not content with fixed doctrines or moral platitudes, many people see themselves as having embarked on personally contoured spiritual voyages. Uncertain of their eventual religious mooring but certain it will not be in a top-heavy religious institution, countless people in North America seek the discovery of dynamic assurance.

This is more than a matter of believing in terms of clinging to fixed certainties. As much as they are in search of belief, many people are just as pushed forward by the urge to belong. More than a set of ideas they can affirm, they look for a group of people with whom new and life-giving experiences can be shaped. They look for grounding in faith tradition and so are intensely curious to be informed. But the information they seek must have shared, practical application. It must also bond them together in worthwhile purpose.

Today's spiritual voyagers want to learn together in small groups, to be enlivened together through inspiring worship, and to serve individuals in need together in homeless shelters, soup kitchens, tutoring programs, and more. The world's needs and opportunities become glaring when you see them through spiritual lenses. Faith can ponder them for only so long; action must result. When people build genuine bonds of faith, healing possibility arises for all. This is the sort of emergence many people today are pursuing.

Although this pursuit has important historical precedent, it is also taking novel form. The blend of faith and community with spirituality and reform reflects past movements. But now its scope is much wider. Given the unprecedented pluralism of American life, emergence has remarkable breadth. The options for spiritual search and faith belonging are dizzying. The result is that "spiritual growth," an historic intent, has become a diverse pursuit. Its sources are varied, its outcomes are multiple. It is not constrained by historic bounds of religious institutions. Consistently this search entails the pursuit of lively faith community across old boundaries. Spiritual dynamism must be found in a group of people who welcome you into their midst regardless of the particular beliefs or faith backgrounds among them. In fact a broad framework for belonging is the necessary feature.

Increasingly American congregations see people on such spiritual voyages at their doors. Many are young adults, but people of all ages surface as spiritual seekers. They seek innovative worship and prayer. They gravitate to discussion groups and educational forums. They surface questions and personal issues that have been mulled deeply and are framed broadly. Now they seek faith perspective. They want to know what to do and how things work in this particular congregation. They care little for its wider religious institution or affiliations. They seek the immediacy of belonging.

Thus they invariably are friendly. They also are impatient. If they sense a congregation is not responsive, or simply invokes what they take to be religious formulas, they vanish and go elsewhere. They are on spiritual voyages that cannot be constrained by what they take to be inertia in a congregation. The energy they bring must soon be matched by energy they encounter. They will continue to search until they find the right circumstance. If no congregation works, they will seek to create their own group for discussion and spiritual journey together.

Often the right circumstance for the spiritual voyagers means an idiosyncratic blend of religious, spiritual, and psychological sources and expressions. Through blending varied streams people seek to discover a deep sense of inner purpose, to surface their gifts and to formulate substantive personal vocation. The great learning of the moment is that this pursuit requires people to step out of individualism and into the creation of community. To do this, people now look broadly at various religious sources. This new receptivity means that "difference" need not be cause for suspicion. Difference can even be celebrated as diverse sources of guidance and points of spiritual insight that have personal application. There is widespread fascination with Buddhism, now seen as a pacific way, or with yoga as a Hindu practice, in congregations of all sorts. Jewish mysticism draws interest, and Muslim prayer offers vivid points of comparison. Many American spiritual pilgrims find "difference" can be enlivening.

For congregations seeking to be both more grounded in their own confession and more attuned to today's spiritual searches, there is no inherent contradiction. Indeed the very theme of difference pervades the sacred texts of the Abrahamic faiths. For centuries each of these faith traditions has been compelled to deal with the presence of the "other" in its midst. How have people who are different been viewed? The answer is encouraging. The sacred texts reveal far more receptivity and fascination than one may assume.

A basic example for all three faiths is found in Genesis chapter 18:

> The Lord appeared to Abraham by the oaks of Mamre, as he sat at the entrance of his tent in the heat of the day. [2]He looked up and saw three men standing near him. When he saw them, he ran from the tent entrance to meet them, and bowed down to the ground. [3]He said, "My lord, if I find favor with you, do not pass by your servant. [4]Let a little water be brought, and wash your feet, and rest yourselves under the tree. [5]Let me bring a little bread, that you may refresh yourselves, and after that you may pass on—since you have come to your servant." So they said, "Do as you have said." [6]And Abraham hastened into the tent to Sarah, and said, "Make ready quickly three measures of choice flour, knead it, and make cakes." [7]Abraham ran to the herd, and took a calf, tender and good, and gave it to the servant, who hastened to prepare it. [8]Then he took curds and milk and the calf that he had prepared, and set it before them; and he stood by them under the tree while they ate.
>
> [9]They said to him, "Where is your wife Sarah?" And he said, "There, in the tent." [10]Then one said, "I will surely return to you in due season, and your wife Sarah shall have a son." And Sarah was listening at the tent entrance behind him. [11]Now Abraham and Sarah were old, advanced in age; it had ceased to be with Sarah after the manner of women. [12]So Sarah laughed to herself, saying, "After I have grown old, and my husband is old, shall I have pleasure?" [13]The Lord said to Abraham, "Why did Sarah laugh, and say, 'Shall I indeed bear a child, now that I am old?' [14]Is anything too wonderful for the Lord? At the set time I will return to you, in due season, and Sarah shall have a son." [15]But Sarah denied, saying, "I did not laugh"; for she was afraid. He said, "Oh yes, you did laugh."

The message of this story is clear. The strangers were emissaries of God, though Abraham did not at first recognize this fact. He ran to greet them though he did not know them. He offered them hospitality, and the result was that Abraham and Sarah discovered an unexpected possibility for new life. In this text those who are different bring possibility that would not be recognized if we ignored them or treated them rudely.

The passage is repeated for added emphasis in the Christian Bible. Hebrews 13:2 encourages the Christian community not to forget to show hospitality to strangers, for by doing so "some have entertained angels without knowing it." However, the central Christian statement on dealing with difference arises in the parable of the good Samaritan, found in Luke 10.

> [29]But wanting to justify himself, he asked Jesus, "And who is my neighbor?" [30]Jesus replied, "A man was going down from Jerusalem to Jericho, and fell into the hands of robbers, who stripped him, beat him, and went away, leaving him half dead. [31]Now by chance a priest was going down that road; and when he saw him, he passed by on the other side. [32]So likewise a Levite, when he came to the place and saw him, passed by on the other side. [33]But a Samaritan while traveling came near him; and when he saw him, he was moved with pity. [34]He went to him and bandaged his wounds, having poured oil and wine on them. Then he put him on his own animal, brought him to an inn, and took care of him. [35]The next day he took out two denarii, gave them to the innkeeper, and said, 'Take care of him; and when I come back, I will repay you whatever more you spend.' [36]Which of these three, do you think, was a neighbor to the man who fell into the hands of the robbers?" [37]He said, "The one who showed him mercy." Jesus said to him, "Go and do likewise."

The Samaritans were people of a different religion and culture. They faced discrimination in the world of Jesus's day. At other points in the Christian texts the Samaritans are actually criticized for their beliefs. But being different, religiously or culturally, did not matter in the face of social challenge. Indeed the Samaritan who paused to help an injured man is praised above persons of accepted religious office. The Samaritan embodies the intent of Jesus's message, and not only on this occasion. John 4 describes how a Samaritan woman gives Jesus water to drink when he is thirsty. The result is that the difference between Samaritans and Christians is noted but fades when there is a common commitment to acts of hospitality and service.

Similar sentiments arise in the Qur'an, this time with special affirmation of Jews and Christians as "people of the Book." Notable examples include Sura 4:36:

> Worship Allah and associate nothing with Him, and to parents do good, and to relatives, orphans, the needy, the near neighbor, the neighbor farther away, the companion at your side, the traveler, and those whom your right hands possess.

In terms of the other Abrahamic faiths, Sura 3:64 is worth noting:

> Say, "O People of the Scripture, come to a word that is equitable between us and you—that we will not worship except Allah and not associate anything with Him and not take one another as lords instead of Allah."

To be sure, profound differences remain. Abraham is not a simple common denominator. Each tradition sees Abraham in terms of its own intentions. But the three faiths agree on him as a precursor, and this opens the door to a typological approach to sacred texts and traditions. That is, a correspondence can be found between the details of a scriptural story and contemporary experience. There are hints of just such an approach in sacred texts, in the words of Jesus, for example. At a time when spiritual searches create the context for many discussions across historic differences, and even among differences within congregations, there is an unusual receptivity. People are seeking common ground on which to build common practice, if not complete agreement on all theological details. The way to face difference constructively requires that we reframe the practices we build on our beliefs. The challenge is as hopeful as it appears awkward: by going deeper into our own faith we can create receptivity to persons of other faiths. We turn now to a discussion of the means by which we take this step: reframing.

REFRAMING FAITH AND LIFE

Framing refers to the meaning we attach to a situation, or a person. It is the image we attach, as we have seen. Think of the frame you create when you take a picture. On what do you focus and why? What sorts of pictures do you take because there are memories you wish to preserve? On the other hand, what gets pushed to the edge of your frame, or is left out entirely? And what might you miss? Inevitably the way we frame a situation means that certain people and things are included, perhaps because they are familiar and appealing and because we want to preserve them as they are. By means of the frames we create, we communicate what we value and what we do not value.

Our values and our frames are not created by rational decision, or even fully consciously. More often our framing reflects a deeply psychological instinct. This basic instinct is activated when we encounter difference. What represents difference can be as basic as a food we have never tried or a place we have never visited before. Then our framing becomes further awakened when we encounter something or someone in our familiar places who is different.

It can be the new family down the street that does not look like the people we know in the neighborhood. Or it can be the young adult visitor to the congregation. She is dressed differently and appears to bring a different style and situation than we're accustomed to seeing. Or in a nearby shop we hear people speaking a language we don't understand. Or a new clerk in the grocery speaks with an accent and is dressed in fabrics that are unfamiliar. Little details such as these accumulate and leave the impression that our familiar haunts are changing. Our habitual way of framing even familiar places no longer fits. Other people are appearing in the picture, and we struggle with whether or how to acknowledge them on what we consider to be our turf. If we include them, what happens to our familiar world?

Framing is how we see the world and how we make sense of the world, what we experience and how we express our perceptions. Given the basic, emotional nature of framing, our instinct is to create dichotomies. We see people and situations in terms of good or bad, like or dislike, right or wrong, agree or disagree, full or empty, and so forth. Day by day we make countless either/or judgments, most of which are necessary and innocent. There are choices to be made at the grocery, or when we purchase clothing, for instance. Most options must be set aside; only a few will appeal and still fewer make it home with us.

It is another matter when we extend either/or thinking to people. Where there is obvious difference, the judgments we are likely to make are obvious: we will disapprove, and not always silently. But is this an approach worthy of people of faith? Can faith communities truly believe that they are fulfilling the dictates of faith by judging people who are different harshly simply because of perceived differences? How does a rejection of difference square with Abraham, who rushed to greet strangers, or with Jesus, who praised Samaritans, or with the Qur'an endorsing love for one's neighbor in general and "People of the Book" in particular? How can either/or thinking be justified in terms of faith?

Unfortunately such thinking frequently arises in faith communities. Each faith is prone to exclusivist thinking: either you accept specific precepts and act in certain ways or you are left out. Such thinking defines the "culture wars" gulf between progressives and traditionalists, as I have noted. But is this really true to the core message of the Abrahamic faiths? Can love of God and love of neighbor be framed as an either/or?

Biblical scholar Peter Ochs challenges either/or thinking as a product of the modern world and not of the original, scriptural thinking.[1] Instead sacred texts pose opportunities, not obstacles, for people to come together. Sacred texts motivate changed lives; they do not consign people to inevitable fates. Ochs sees the intention of making connections to God and to other people as the major purpose of these texts and of the traditions they inspire. The goal of creating relation, if we take it to heart, reframes our approach to scripture and to other people. Instead of accepting unbridgeable difference from people of whom we are suspicious, there is the prospect of a bridge appearing. Lest we hesitate to test it, the scripture texts prove clear: like Abraham we must rush to greet the stranger. Their arrival in our midst brings the prospect of new life.

The result is that we reframe a situation when we shift from speaking of "them" to speaking of "us," from "they" to "we." Different points of view and different values and styles hold the prospect of different perspectives, abilities, and energies becoming available. Instead of competition there can be teamwork. Instead of conflict, discernment together can encourage consensus. This turn fulfills the most basic teaching of our scriptures.

But such a turn may not be easy. Lingering suspicion fueled by fearful images can be hard to overcome. Such images pervade the news media and infect our social circles. Blaming a particular group or faith or political outlook makes a complex situation seem easy to understand. Reframing introduces multidimensional realities that defy easy assumptions. Seeing difference accurately, we can no longer be content with stereotypes and suspicions. In the face of difference we must learn how to live together.

In *The Righteous Mind*, Jonathan Haidt suggests how this can happen.[2] A scholar of neuroscience and social behavior, he concludes that human beings have an innate capacity for making connections with others, even people who are different. For connections to happen, what Haidt calls "the hive switch" must be activated. Each person has the capacity, under the right circumstances, to step across what otherwise divides. The hive switch is a basic recognition of a common humanity, which people naturally wish to accomplish. It is an innate moral sense.

It is also an innate social sense. People want to form groups, Haidt says, and not just groups like themselves. Human beings are biologically created to transcend themselves and to build shared purpose. In a word, people have a natural capacity for *empathy*. This is the ability to "walk in someone else's shoes," that is, to see and feel the world as someone else does. What is more likely to surface this capacity than any other source, Haidt concludes, is religion.

Rather than rejection of difference or avoidance of it, the Abrahamic faiths encourage recognition of common human needs. Hospitality to the stranger figures prominently in the scriptures, given the harsh climate and limited resources of the ancient Middle East. The stranger is a person who does not belong to one's own group or even to a group that is recognized. But that is of little consideration when one needs food (Hebrews 13) or protection (Judges 19). Recognition of common human experience and common challenges must draw people together. The faith traditions encourage what human beings are naturally wired to achieve. The moral codes posed in sacred texts offer a path to building community among all people. *Empathy*, the recognition of a basic human unity and possibility, is the doorway. We must see that because we face common challenges with people who are different from us, we can find common direction.

We begin to find common direction by remembering the basic affirmation people of faith share: love of God and love of neighbor. These basic tenets unite Islam and Christianity and Judaism. They also are basic to people of the same faith who otherwise differ, and people in the same congregation who find they are divided. But how closely could these affirmations draw you toward people who are different? The answer is that we can go a long way by returning to our basic affirmations in the face of common challenges. The differences are genuine but so are the similarities and the challenges. How can we emphasize these parallels to enhance our capacity to understand one another? When we list our challenges, we see that we stand on similar ground.

Culture

Let's consider issues that face the three Abrahamic faiths. As you do, you can begin to see that the same issues impact your faith tradition and likely your congregation as well. The relation of faith to culture is complex, especially now when there is much in daily life that gives faithful people pause. All three Abrahamic faiths uphold certain moments in time when religion and culture blended well. All three intend to ground themselves in cultural settings sufficiently to live their convictions faithfully. Yet all three can find themselves at odds with some of the values linked to a given culture. All three offer moral direction that is at odds with the world.

All three faiths share misgivings about aspects of the contemporary world. Within each faith there are people concerned about the environment, about poverty and economic inequalities, and about injustice. Religious people who trace their identity to the prophets, beginning with Abraham, share a lineage of concern about living the faith in circumstances that can challenge belief. The need for political and social reform in some settings, and the spread of secular disdain for religion in others, represent common cultural challenges to the Abrahamic faiths. Even at the level of the congregation, this challenge can be apparent. The outreach programs of congregations are often responses to the impact of culture upon individual lives.

Compassion

Several years ago, at an interfaith conference sponsored by the government of a Middle East country, common ground among the Abrahamic faiths surfaced quickly. Though differences in their theological and historical approaches surfaced, all three gave strong emphasis to an ethic of compassion. All have long legacies of providing aid to people in need, including the sick, the hungry, and the homeless. The importance of medicine is apparent, and many believers are drawn to careers in the health professions. This means that the Abrahamic faiths share two core commitments: an emphasis on human well-being and an emphasis on service to create the conditions of well-being. Islam's emphasis on charity makes clear the nature of its commitment and readily finds parallels in the other faiths.

There are both shared and unique features of the emphasis on health. Both Judaism and Islam reject eating pork, for example, and both only eat other kinds of meat that have been prepared according to certain religious guidelines. "Halal" foods for Muslims thus prove similar to "kosher" foods for Jews. There are differences. Islam firmly teaches abstinence from alcohol consumption while some Jews and Christians voluntarily take this step.

On the whole all three faiths teach respect for life and take active steps to promote health. All three align themselves with current medical research and practice. The theme of compassion taps the highest ideals of each and can be a principal avenue of cooperation.

Education

We have noted Islam's emphasis on education, and we have cited the unparalleled youth of many parts of the Muslim world. It should also be clear that Christians and Jews share these traits in their own ways. Two challenges arise from these realities. First, faith communities of all sorts face the challenge of educating young people in the faith at a time when their population is young to an unprecedented extent. Second, faithful people and historic faith communities of all sorts face the growth of independent voices and groups claiming to speak for the faith. Fueled by Internet and media access, a variety of individuals, groups, and even movements have multiplied in each of the Abrahamic faiths. Each faith has given rise to television preachers, websites, and blogs.

The challenge for all three faiths is that a bewildering variety of messages and figures have surfaced, many focused narrowly on bits of religious tradition lifted beyond the faith's original intention and breadth. The obvious example is fundamentalism and its extremist offshoots. Within themselves and together, the three faiths face the challenge of forging consensus and applying consensus to further the issues they face. But building consensus is the heart of their challenge. In the next section we discuss the path to understanding among people who are different.

THE PATH TO UNDERSTANDING

> Blessed Lord, Who caused all holy scriptures to be written for our learning: Grant us so to hear them, read, mark, learn, and inwardly digest them, that we may embrace and ever hold fast the blessed hope of everlasting life, which you have given us in our Savior Jesus Christ; who lives and reigns with you and the Holy Spirit; one God, for ever and ever. Amen.
>
> —*The Book of Common Prayer*, the Episcopal Church

Culture, compassion, and education are broad illustrations of the challenges all faith traditions now face. Exclusivist movements within their own ranks and fault lines over moral and social issues are also common to all faith communities. But if there are similar challenges, can there be a common response? Can differences be bridged when people of faith have such a basis for unity? This does not mean that differences can be eliminated; it means that faith traditions can build understanding of their common challenges and affirmations in ways that encourage common possibility.

Jonathan Sacks emphasizes the importance of this step. As a rabbi, he speaks out of Judaism's capacity to welcome strangers and to honor the distinctive wisdom of all religions. In *The Dignity of Difference* he cites the common ethical base of the three Abrahamic faiths, "though each speaks in its own distinctive accent."[3] Each religion insists upon respect for the stranger, even though suspicion of difference has dominated history. People of faith are called to differentiate themselves, that is, to welcome people whom society would prefer to disregard. This is especially needed in an age of globalization. Sacks emphasizes that in thirty-six different places the Hebrew Bible commands love of the stranger.

This emphasis echoes across the faith traditions. As a result, one question sums up our challenge: how can common affirmations of different faith traditions be gathered up and made plain, to unite people? Fortunately there are impressive resources for seeing clearly the scriptural command to love others, even the stranger, and to find common ground through holy scriptures. In the face of difference, people are gathering to find understanding.

A foremost example is "Scriptural Reasoning," a process of reading the sacred texts of Muslims, Christians, and Jews. In a small group, guided by "bundled" texts that speak to key themes of faith, there is open-ended discussion. The goal is to build understanding and mutual appreciation. The assumption is that common ground will emerge, though the actual path to it must be charted by the group. Themes which could become the focus of discussion could include human nature, wisdom, education and knowledge, women and equality, and so forth.

Created at the University of Cambridge with an important center at the University of Virginia, Scriptural Reasoning has sound footing.[4] But its intention is more than academic. "SR" intends to encourage creative vulnerability and hospitality among its participants. Vulnerability arises in part from allowing persons of a different faith to assess texts from your own tradition. Vulnerability also arises from an open-ended approach that creates a measure of uncertainty. The atmosphere, however, is not critical but hospitable. There is an inherent effort to discover and an assumption of common affirmation.

The affirmation Scriptural Reasoning pursues is no unspecified agreement. A larger belief pervades its energy. Put simply, there is a conviction that the sacred texts of the three faiths all reveal the truth and goodness of God. Each scripture states God's proclamation, the divine intention for human beings. Thus, in Judaism, the basic declaration is the *Shema*: "Hear O Israel, the Lord your God is one God." In Islam, the basic declaration is the *Shahada*: "There is one God and Muhammad is his prophet." Similarly, for Christians, the basic proclamation is Jesus's summary of ancient law: "'Love the Lord your God with all your heart and with all your soul and with all your mind.' This is the first and great commandment. And the second is like it: 'Love your neighbor as yourself.'"

In turn the basic role of a believer is to be a witness to these affirmations. The believer is a person who has felt the presence of God and who finds necessary understanding of God in the living affirmation of faith tradition. Any discussion of sacred texts cannot remain abstract if it is to be faithful. People who gather to explore texts are opening up their personal experience of God. The vulnerability of which Scriptural Reasoning speaks is a most basic, human openness to speaking of God. It is also a critical openness to discovering different experiences of God in the lives of other people. As Peter Ochs, one of the creators of SR, has noted, it is not a case of one approach being right or better or truer. All traditions bear witness to God. From out of our different perceptions and convictions, common relation becomes possible. This bond in the midst of difference is the goal, and the open-ended nature of SR allows diverse people to find that bond together.

Of course differing experiences of God not only surface among Jews, Muslims, and Christians. The differences and the similarities are large among the Abrahamic faiths. But even within one faith—among Christians, for instance—there are profoundly different experiences of God. Consider the differences between evangelicals and Roman Catholics, for example. Yet it is crucial to recall that each form of Christian faith, like each expression of Judaism or Islam, presents a precious vision of divine truth.

In each expression, God is present and believers are called to respond. This simple realization surfaces in all forms of religious life. It is present in congregations and can easily shape the dynamics of congregational life. In adult forums and scripture study groups, the purpose is to understand sacred texts and to bring God's reality more vividly into our lives and the activities of our families and communities. But very different experiences of God soon surface when discussion becomes substantial. It can be startling and loom as a threat to group unity. But if people stay at the table and listen, and resist either/or approaches, a remarkable bond can grow among the group.

Members of congregations can readily attest to how such bonds grow out of the soil of difference. Likely your congregation is familiar with one or another program or curriculum or discussion group for the study of scripture, or the knowledge of sacred tradition. Likely you also have been trained to serve in one or another program of a congregation, where you have awakened to your own experience of God, and to the variety of perceptions of God among other people in the group.

But as you learn, a remarkable unity takes shape. In the group context you learn, and through learning you are encouraged to live more fully into the life of faith as your own tradition has articulated it. The full meaning of relation comes into focus: each one of us must live into a particular tradition and a particular faith community, the truth of which deepens our experience of God's truth. Yet at the same time, as we go deeply into our own tradition, ultimately we are called to affirm the experiences of others, however different they may be.

In the next chapter we explore what this process of going deeper into particularity, yet becoming open to all, looks like. Our goal is to build understanding of difference, and through understanding to create a basis for cooperation. We can be transformed by each other's wisdom, and so drawn into bonds of appreciation and common purpose. This is because, however different, each of our experiences is from God.

QUESTIONS FOR DISCUSSION

1. Have you ever offered hospitality and received an unexpected gift or opportunity as a result?
2. When have you felt closely connected to another person? How was your "hive switch," as Haidt calls it, activated? How was a connection created?
3. When and how have you moved deeper in your faith? How did it happen? How did your life change as a result?

INDIVIDUAL AND GROUP EXERCISES

1. Select one of the three Abrahamic faiths. What different groups or "denominations" exist within the faith you selected? What is the reason for such "difference" within one faith tradition?
2. What does it mean to be grounded in a faith tradition? If we are all searching for God, does it matter how we do it?
3. Encounters with difference can be threatening because they make us feel uncertain about our own faith. Think of a time when this has happened to you. Many theories suggest the human instinct is "fight or flight" in the face of a perceived threat. Has the presence of difference caused you to consider "fight" or "flight"?
4. It is hard to live with ambiguity, in "gray" areas. When it is not clearly a good or a bad situation, we can feel paralyzed, with no clear direction. Think of a time in your life that was gray, with no

clear direction and perhaps no clear resolution. How did you handle such ambiguity?

5. Empathy is the ability to walk in someone else's shoes. Think of the first time you were aware of the feelings of another person, especially if they diverged from your own feelings. How did this happen? Was this discovery related to your faith or to your faith community? How could congregations do better at encouraging empathy?

LEARNING FROM OTHER FAITHS

What is love? Define love in three faith groups.

SCRIPTURE LESSON

"Jesus said, 'I am the way, and the truth, and the life.'" (John 14:6).

How does this scripture help you make decisions when you encounter difference? How does it help you in the gray areas of life?

PRAY

All traditions bear witness to God. Pray that your own traditions bear witness to God, not to yourselves.

7

MISSION AND THE COMMON GOOD

AT AN INTERFAITH MEETING

As he sat at the small table, Tony felt a level of discomfort he did not like. It was an odd sort of feeling that made him wonder whether he should leave abruptly or quietly pay closer attention. As he debated with himself about giving in to his feelings or being dutiful, a man in casual dress with a long beard was explaining something about his faith that made little sense to Tony. Nor was Tony sure that he cared. When he surveyed the faces around the table, Tony wondered why they were there. He was sure that the only reason he had come was because his minister asked him to attend. That thought dissolved as his mind drifted back to work and then to an errand he promised his wife he would do. He was tempted to jot a note to himself: "Must not forget to make that stop," he mused. If this meeting lasted too long, he would have to excuse himself and leave.

It occurred to Tony that several people at the table seemed friendly when he arrived. His mind was drifting back toward the meeting, and he noted the man in the black suit and clerical collar who had greeted him at the door. A woman had offered coffee from a tray of cups. Another man, in a knit yarmulke, had made a quip about this being the place to come for prayer, all sorts of prayer. Tony smiled but still felt awkward as the meeting began. It was nice that so many churches, if that's what they were, could meet. But what would be the result? Tony was not sure who or what could bring this group together; they were all so different. There was little sense of what they had in common, other than being at the table. Anyway, he had enough to do already, at home and at church.

His mind again adrift, Tony knew he had a congregational committee meeting to chair later that week and struggled to recall when it had been scheduled. He resolved to check his calendar and briefly scolded himself for being unsure. An important meeting loomed, a meeting where the purpose was quite clear. His congregation's youth director had resigned suddenly. That wasn't all bad, he rationalized; she seemed to have run out of new ideas and now was getting married and moving to another city. But that would mean a search for a new director, if the budget would allow them to hire one. Tony sighed and shifted in his seat. This would mean more work at his own congregation, much less doing anything with these others. And that would be on top of his job and his family. He did not have time for this other thing, whatever this meeting was. And he had to run that errand for his wife, because he forgot to do it yesterday. And with that thought his resolve to leave the meeting politely but firmly was set. The only question now was finding the right moment.

Tony must have sighed too loudly and contorted his face too obviously. A woman in a clergy shirt looked at him, smiled, and spoke: "You don't seem to like the idea. What would you do? Are we missing something? Oh, sorry, I'm Laura, from the Lutheran church down the street. Don't you think we should have a Jewish-Muslim-Christian Thanksgiving service?"

Tony was caught flat-footed. His distractions were no longer concealed. But the man in the yarmulke saved him further embarrassment. "Look, of course he's for it. He's here. And it's a good idea. All of us teach about hospitality. This town needs to get together, around something we can agree on. Who's against Thanksgiving? We'll pray and have a reception together. Oh yes, I'm Jeff, from the congregation across town." He extended his hand to Tony, who shook it gratefully. "Hi everyone, I'm Tony." Now he felt embarrassed and in the spotlight.

But maybe it was Laura's smile or Jeff's helpful intervention and handshake. Or maybe the image of different people together for Thanksgiving touched a thoughtful place in Tony. All of a sudden this evening began to make sense to him. It was shifting from a vague gathering of different people and a distraction from the really important things and people. Although he did not know or understand these people, suddenly there was something compelling. For one thing, they had become people with names and smiles. Whatever they believed or did, there was a dawn of possibility in being with them. Still awkward, but now relaxing, Tony took another step forward. "We should have a Thanksgiving service. And our Presbyterian church will help."

"Great," said the man with the long beard. "And I am Malik, from the Islamic center." He extended his hand as well, which Tony gratefully accepted. But now his head was spinning: Jews, Muslims, and all sorts of Christians, even a Catholic priest. Why had his minister asked him to attend this meeting? Well, it was surprising; maybe because they all seemed nice; maybe because they weren't arguing and found something basic to do together. The idea made sense, he mused; okay, he would do what he could to help.

But one more surprise awaited Tony two days later when he spoke with his minister about the meeting. He quipped that "I certainly did not know what was in store for me." His minister chuckled and thanked Tony for attending. "Good job, well done. We need to do more of this. The community is changing and we need to participate more with other faiths. This can really move the mission program of our congregation forward." That word hung in Tony's mind: "mission." He had heard "mission" described in all sorts of ways and had never been clear about what it meant or what he thought it should mean. But "mission" with people of different faiths was a totally new thought.

Tony is not alone. "Mission" with people of different faiths is a new idea indeed. It seemed daunting enough to try to get different Christians together, but having Muslims and Jews, as well as all sorts of Christians, seemed impossible. Well, Tony thought, they had little trouble agreeing on a Thanksgiving service. "But should mission mean converting other people to my belief?" he wondered. Tony was not comfortable with that thought, but he could not dismiss it. He did not like the idea of pressuring someone, of trying to force people to do something. On the other hand, mission suggested you really believed in something and were clear about it. What did the minister mean? Was it really mission if you were working in collaboration with people who were different?

The word "mission" is often used in congregations. In Tony's case it was clear that mission had little to do with evangelism, or trying to convert people to Christianity, or to his own denomination. Mission in

Tony's case referred vaguely to their overall purpose as a congregation, although this too was not clear. It occurred to Tony that they had housed homeless people, and there was a tutoring program, and a group had gone to Honduras to see if they could help after a tropical storm. That sounded like mission. Tony felt better, assured that his own congregation was doing something. But he was still confused about mission. It felt like something was missing from his congregation.

Something was missing, for Tony and for his congregation. That was both good and bad. Confusion about mission was not good, because it meant the congregation was confused about their identity and purpose. But attending an interfaith meeting, and speaking with the minister, and wondering what mission meant was filled with potential. For Christians, mission has been central in several respects. Now, in the face of difference, mission must acquire new meaning, for congregations especially, who face difference in their neighborhoods. Increasingly mission entails deepening one's own faith and life as a faith community, while building creative ties to people of other faiths. It sounded like a contradiction, and it was no wonder Tony felt confusion. How can your congregation both build itself up and build up others? And yet, as Tony began to sense, through such ties effective benefits for the life of local communities become possible. This can happen, if we reframe the meaning of mission.

For a large segment of the world's Christians mission has meant, and continues to mean, conversion. The expansion of Christianity around the world rested on the dedicated work of missionaries who brought multitudes to Christ. The work of Christians around the world to serve countless numbers in schools and hospitals has often grown out of the impetus to convert as many as possible. Many Christians assume there is no purpose for meeting with people of other faiths than to try to convert them, even people from other branches of Christianity. The challenge of dealing with religious difference is simply to dissolve it through conversion. There can be no other approach, no other priority.

Tony's congregation, like many others, resists the notion that simply converting others is being faithful or effective in facing difference. "We're not like them," Tony found himself saying, nodding toward an evangelical congregation across the street. The image of pressuring people did not square with his faith. But talk of mission made him and other lay leaders in his congregation nervously uncertain. They could agree that mission meant helping people in need. They could generate energy and money for that. Beyond that, they were not clear, except for what they did not want to do, namely, be like the evangelical congregation.

About one thing Tony and his colleagues could be sure: for many Christians past and present mission has meant response to human need, not conditioned on how they respond to pressure to convert. To be sure, the hope of conversion can surface when someone shows a flicker of interest in Christianity. But many Christians find sufficient integrity and effectiveness in their faith when they serve people's basic needs, especially feeding, clothing, healing, housing, and educating. The legacy of such service is profound, and it continues today. In much of the world, many hospitals and clinics and schools and colleges have Christian origins. Over the past generation there has been a surge of new schools founded in congregations. Today, as for centuries, Christian mission means service.

At times in the past such efforts have united Christians of various denominations. The original Protestant "Sunday schools" in the early nineteenth century grew out of collaboration among different Christian traditions. Difference of theology and worship faded in the face of common opportunities and challenges. As new American cities grew, there was an obvious need for basic education and grounding in basic religious precepts on which there was agreement. Put in practical terms, for children to read the Bible, they first had to learn to read. For children to complete basic school lessons, they had to be able to write and to count. Basic education was needed to learn the faith. Cooperation to offer education arose across lines of difference.

Eventually such collaboration faded. Each denomination concluded that Sunday schools should present not only basic Christian beliefs, but specific forms of belief and practice. In a sense, mission as conversion to a particular identity took over. The reason was not simply to compete with other traditions: with some justification denominational leaders feared the loss of their tradition's identity. They worried that lack of clarity would do more harm than good. The result was increased competition for several generations, until new opportunities for cooperation arose. Difference can neither be ignored nor overcome. While being clear about your identity, you must build bridges to those whose faith identity is different. It can begin, if people of different faiths simply gather to consider what they can do together.

THE TOUGHEST ISSUE OF ALL

"So what do I tell my membership," the minister of a large evangelical congregation asked his interfaith colleagues at a luncheon. "How do I explain to them why we are meeting, because to most of them the only valid reason for me to be here is to convert you." A minister from a Protestant congregation that was not evangelical chuckled, but his evangelical friend did not hesitate. "Oh my friend, they mean you too. To them you are not fully Christian."

A Jewish rabbi at the table shook his head vigorously, but a Muslim imam smiled mischievously. "It's simple," the imam said. "Just tell the leaders of your congregation that you've become a Muslim!" The response brought nervous laughter around the table. It was a sign of rare openness and acceptance among this group of interfaith clergy. But it was also a sign of the importance and delicacy of mission. No theme so reveals the core principles of each faith, nor the complex and unresolved history among faiths. No theme is a more ready source of rivalry and conflict. Mission is also a theme that surfaces internal divisions among Christians, as well as among Jews and Muslims. Mission divides as profoundly as it can unite.

There are prominent examples of assertiveness related to mission. Evangelical Christianity is energetically focused on conversion with little regard for understanding or cooperation apart from this goal. Conversion is the prism through which all interfaith light must filter. But to other American Christians, mission generally has a somewhat different appeal: amid conflict and uncertainty in denominations and congregations, mission looms as a sign of fresh unity and purpose. It offers the promise of tangible activities and results. These results may not be measured by numbers of people converted, but it could be defined by numbers served or taught or trained or fed. Often mission is measured internally, by numbers of people, or numbers of committee meetings, and volumes of e-mails and minutes from those meetings. The lure of mission is its relation to concrete activities that appear to energize a divided faith community and to diminish its fragmentation. Mission can become a rallying cry.

Of course there are numerous examples, historically and in the present, of highly assertive approaches to mission by all of the Abrahamic faiths, and among Christians. In an age of religious pluralism, with increasing numbers of the American population saying "NONE" is their religious affiliation, the incentive to mission is high. "Church planting" by evangelical groups, in North America and on every other continent, is widespread, with highly touted results. Perhaps more than ever, mission initiatives launched by individual congregations seek to convert or to serve unreached people. There are fewer high-profile, denominational mission programs, as there were in past generations. But sheer efforts to reach and to persuade are apparent in every town and city. Measured simply by energy, mission may have reached an unprecedented scale.

But mission in the face of difference must acquire new and actually more profound depth. If one measures mission not simply by initiative and intention, then a more substantive and ultimately more productive meaning to mission awaits people and congregations of all faiths. Considering the relation of Christianity to other religions, Jacques Dupuis, S.J., makes a crucial point: Christians must live fully into their truth, expecting that people who believe differently will do the same, including people of various forms of Christianity itself. The key is not to reject the experience of people who are different, or to think in exclusivist terms. The key is to build a basis first for "dialogue" and then for "common commitment."

Dupuis outlines the components of Christian mission for the contemporary church. He notes that what is new about mission today "is the acute awareness attained by our world of the pluralism of cultures and of religious traditions, and of the right each has to its difference." Inherently based upon respect for difference, mission must include witness, service, prayer and contemplation, and dialogue. Quoting a Vatican statement, "Dialogue and Mission," Dupuis explains that dialogue occurs "when Christians meet the followers of other religious traditions in order to walk together towards truth and to walk together in projects of common concern."

Mission by Christians must include genuine proclamation and witness. But this takes a form that is broad without diminishing Christian conviction and confession. Dialogue and common witness are based in the agreement that God's work of salvation has a broad footprint, visible across lines that would otherwise divide. In fact, there is an expectation, and even a need, for different faiths to proclaim their convictions. If the lines of difference surface plainly among Christians, or even within a single congregation, one must still assume that difference cannot be glossed over. Difference is genuine, and it surfaces. But, to learn from Dupuis and the Roman Catholic view, difference requires dialogue and "projects of common concern." One must stand fully within one's own truth and honor others as they stand within the truth they proclaim.

Notably, key concepts like "proclamation" and "witness" become crucial for Jews and Muslims as well as Christians. The Shahada is Islam's basic confession: "There is one God and Muhammad is His Prophet." A shahid in Arabic is someone who has become a "witness," a person who has laid down his life to fulfill a religious commandment (Sura 16:89). Similarly, the Muslim concept of Dawah refers to the preaching of Islam. It is an invitation or summons to understand Islam, and perhaps to join its affirmation. One who issues such an invitation is, in effect, a missionary. Also similar, the basic Jewish affirmation is the Shema Yisrael: "Hear O Israel, the Lord is One God." Through recitation of the Shema one becomes a living witness testifying to the truth of this tradition, and to its continuation.

By the very wording of these basic affirmations, the common basis of the Abrahamic faiths becomes clear, and a model is suggested for how religious difference can yield common ground, even among people of the same faith and the same congregation. In the face of any instance of religious difference, the search for basic, common proclamation will likely prove fruitful. It will also be important to note that making such witness is a common impulse. Such recognition is crucial to a basic shift in outlook that is necessary: from emphasis on difference or division and discord, there must be a turn toward emphasis on common affirmation, from emphasis on exclusivity to emphasis on inclusivity. It is possible to give witness to one's own faith and to affirm the witness of people who are different. This occurs in the context of dialogue and projects of common concern. One can surrender zero-sum thinking, turning instead to the realization that difference enhances; it need not incite competition.

How can this begin? For one leader named Becky, it came as a realization at a retreat for the mission committee of her congregation. She went to the retreat reluctantly, distressed by the level of division in the pews and at meetings. There were long and difficult conversations among the membership. Subgroups gathered in the parking lot; cliques spoke by e-mail and phone. Becky assumed these differences were irreconcilable; the people involved seemed angry and rigid. There appeared to be scant hope of finding common ground. She left for the retreat trying to be hopeful but with misgivings. She had to admit, she was suspicious of some of the people who would attend the retreat.

The retreat introduced a provocative but surprising question for the group's day together: when have you felt close to God in your congregation? The question startled Becky and at first seemed like a distraction to her. When would the group move to discussing the issues of the congregation and the sort of mission programs they should build? It was fine to talk about God; but shouldn't they simply pray and perhaps have some silence to gather themselves? Prayer and silence would be ample preparation for the work they needed to do. Time was short. They knew why they were there. How they would overcome their differences was not at all clear; but they needed every minute to try.

The retreat leader had given them some paper on which to jot any notes, and then to share something of what they had realized. There was silence and obvious hesitation. Clearly this was not a typical conversation for this group. It was apparent to Becky that others were hesitant and struggling, just as she was; and this was not the struggle she envisioned for this day. She wondered if she should challenge this approach; she could feel time ticking by. But at last, one person dared to speak.

"Maybe it is just me," he began apologetically, "but if I understand your question to us, the closest I have felt to God in our congregation was when my father died. Our minister came to visit, and to pray. And we had that funeral that I still remember; it gives me goose bumps. My dad had been sick for a long time. I miss him, but after that service, I know that he is at peace with God." He struggled with the last few words, and tears were clearly forming at his eyes' edges. "I didn't really know what I believed until then." He was now fighting back more tears. "But I felt a hope I had never felt before." The group was seated in a circle, and a woman to the man's right reached over to pat his hand. The man on his left put an arm around his shoulder.

Becky shifted nervously but sensed that something unusual and crucial could happen. This could be a different conversation, a thought that was confirmed when another woman began to speak rapidly and nervously. "I don't know if this fits, and maybe it sounds trite now, but when my daughter was in the Christmas pageant, I was so moved. I guess I had felt competitive. I have to admit that. I really wanted my daughter to have a big part. I knew I would be so proud; I'm a single parent, and we have been through so much. But when she was up there, I saw all of those children, looking so wonderful. That taught me something, about God and about us. I mean, we are in this together, aren't we?"

Quickly more accounts surfaced. Some had felt closer to God at a moving worship service. Some felt closer to God when they worked in a homeless shelter. One had been moved by a class; another had been helped by the minister after a divorce. Their paths were different and had been very private. Suddenly the difference faded and the privacy was lowered. In the same congregation, they had all found pathways to God. As they talked, they found themselves bound together in a new way. They were more than members of a certain congregation, more than individuals charged with the work of a committee. In the same place, God had come near to them. God's different approaches to each did not matter; they were now clear that they had shared something life-giving in the same place, and so had something life-giving to share together. They soon realized there was a strong, new basis for leadership of their congregation.

In all three Abrahamic faiths, there is a strong emphasis on theophany, that is, on God coming near. The manner of God's appearing varies widely, but in each case a place becomes sacred because God has been experienced there. Among Jews, of course, Mount Sinai is but one example of a sacred space. For Muslims, the Dome of the Rock in Jerusalem and the Kabba at Mecca represent places where God has been revealed. Christians revere the places Jesus walked, from the Mount of Olives and the Sea of Galilee to Golgotha, the site of his crucifixion and then resurrection.

In similar fashion, for us, as individuals and as families and friends, congregations become sacred places. Often hallways are lined with pictures of key people and events in which we feel a stake. There are memorial plaques with names we know, and even the names of loved ones. Particular rooms, and certainly the sanctuary itself, surface memories of pivotal life moments and times when we were together with people we have loved. Congregations also readily surface painful moments and hurts and confusions; but the congregation always reminds us that there is a faith and a place to turn where unexpected healing becomes possible. Through such moments we become bound, with God and with one another.

So it happened for Becky and for her committee. Each person brought a different story. But the common faith shone through their differences. They sensed that they had been loved and led and healed beyond their ordinary experience, and far beyond any expectations. They gained a sense of being tied together in a place where God had come near, and continued to come near. They gained a joint sense of stewardship for the gifts and possibilities of their congregations and their people. They began to see that mission promised depth and unity and clarity if they could focus less on tasks and more on engaging the personal stories beneath the minutes and agendas.

Embraced at its true depth, mission can lead beyond exclusivity and can inspire unity and cooperation. And when it is genuine, mission dares to look not only at intentions, nor at what the congregation and its own people will gain. For the sake of bridging difference and living fully into the promise of mission, there must also be close attention to the impact upon others, those we would serve. Our ability to unite our congregations does affect our ability to serve others.

TOWARD COMMON MISSION

If mission today is imperative at all levels of religious life, what shape must it take? If there are strong incentives to mission among the Abrahamic faiths, is there also a strong basis for cooperation? How can congregations embrace mission in the hope of both living more fully into their faith and collaborating more substantially with persons of different convictions, within their own flock and beyond? There must be a strong new clarity and initiative in the congregation, to be sure. But there must also be a new, personal dimension. The concept of "recognition" must be at the heart of mission by congregations today.

An obvious example of recognition comes from the world of diplomacy. "Diplomatic recognition" means formal acknowledgment between nations, or acknowledgment by nations, of such ideals as human rights and legal status for minority groups or refugees. Refusal to grant recognition occurs amid conflict or the uncertainty that follows the overthrow of a government. Recognition becomes the beginning of new relations and ties between nations.

This sort of recognition can occur formally among religious organizations of various kinds. For example, in 2000 the Evangelical Lutheran Church in America (ELCA) and the Episcopal Church adopted "Called to Common Mission," a document establishing full communion between them.[1] Under this agreement there was recognition of the validity of each church's baptisms and ordinations. A stumbling block between these churches has been the Episcopal understanding of the office and function of bishops versus the Lutheran view. Adoption of "Called to Common Mission" signaled that recognition was more important than difference. Neither church "converted" to the other's theology of the episcopate; in a sense they agreed to disagree. But such acceptance allowed recognition to take precedence over difference, and an important agreement was achieved.

Much the same could be said of "A Common Word," the historic document released in 2007 as we have noted. Hundreds of leaders of the Abrahamic faiths from around the world, especially Muslims and Christians, have endorsed love of God and love of neighbor as core principles they share. The differences between the faiths are not eliminated, but an impressive act of recognition has occurred. What should have been obvious for a long time has been announced publicly, drawing diverse people together. That they should gather for conversation and for cooperation has broken important ground. "Common mission" can only begin when there is mutual recognition.

It can take courage to break this sort of ground, that is, to offer recognition where there has been not only difference but enmity. Yet such actions prove historic, and even when prompt results are not forthcoming, long-term change has begun. Just such a moment occurred on October 16, 1901, when President Theodore Roosevelt invited African American leader Booker T. Washington to dinner at the White House.

It would be an obvious and perhaps politically necessary gesture now. Washington was a distinguished educator and the author of a book that had gained unusual recognition, since the author represented a race of people only recently enslaved. For some of the American people there was great pride in Washington's accomplishment. *Up from Slavery* gave African Americans hope for eventual equality. Though free in theory, in fact they were mired in discrimination and outright racism. Their possibilities were marginal at best. Apparently struck by the book as a window on American race relations, Roosevelt took the simple step of inviting Washington to dinner.

At the beginning of the twentieth century, however, this was a dangerous political step. Though now painful and even astonishing to recall, white racism was blatant and remorseless, and arose from various quarters of white society. Roosevelt was roundly condemned for what was taken as a foolhardy gesture. Even more "moderate" voices avowed that different races should not meet socially, especially at the White House. The impact of Roosevelt's action was a shadow cast across his political career. He never again invited Washington, or any other African American person, to dinner. Yet he appeared in public with Washington on various occasions, and in 1905 he visited Tuskegee Institute, Washington's pioneering educational initiative in Alabama. Over a century later the recognition Roosevelt accorded Washington, and by extension the hopes of African American people, can be seen as an historic step that foreshadowed later challenges to discrimination based on racial difference.

The simple act of recognition put difference in focus, and mistreatment of people based on difference under scrutiny. This was a new level of attention that many did not want because it forced them to surface their prejudices and to be judged by them. At times such obvious, intense scrutiny is required to eliminate barriers to acceptance of a common humanity. Difference is not erased, and never can or should be. But a common, human basis and common possibilities can triumph.

Today, in most cases, the barriers to common mission by people of different faiths do not reflect the overt racism that was prominent a century ago. Incentives to mission by congregations are now profound, and there is clear awareness that mission entails dealing directly with difference. In part, as I have illustrated, this means coming to grips with differences within the congregation that impede mission, and lifting up a focus on mission that can rally a congregation's leaders. There are signs today that many congregations are achieving sufficient internal focus that their attention on mission produces impressive results. Robert Wuthnow, a sociologist of religion at Princeton University, has paid extended attention to the capacity of religious Americans and their congregations for mission. He has written on acts of compassion, on spirituality, and on kindness arising from religious motivation. In *Boundless Faith*, Wuthnow extends these interests into an analysis of a surprising phenomenon: a dramatic increase since 2000 in the number of congregations that regularly conduct short-term mission trips overseas.[2]

Though a portion of this effort is clearly intended for evangelism, Wuthnow finds that much of it takes humanitarian form. Mission is resolutely tied to service and to deeply spiritual motivations, both personally and in one's congregation. As old-line, national religious institutions have declined, local and congregational efforts have taken off. Mission increasingly means people encountering people for the sake of addressing basic human needs.

Even in the midst of acts of service, however, the deep purpose of mission can be overlooked. A focus on tasks, even of a noble sort, can lose sight of the opportunity for mutual recognition and for discovering common humanity and common purpose. The most apparent trap is institutional process. Congregations, as religious institutions, can succumb to measuring mission by energies applied to the task. Numbers of meetings and even the rapport reached by members of a congregational committee can become the parameters of "success." Likewise, numbers of people served may be closer to the intention of mission, but the people whose lives are bettered can still remain faceless. It becomes tempting for mission teams to function impersonally, even when they offer effective service. Too often, short-term teams retreat to upscale hotels after a day of service, thus preserving an unfortunate separation. It is possible to go on a trip, conduct otherwise admirable service, and never gain the recognition of, nor grant it to, the persons you traveled to be with.

The doorway to recognition of the other person, and so to the true intention of mission in my opinion, begins with a simple question: who has been affected by the presence of people acting for the sake of mission? And how has that influence been felt? In a word, this means: what has been the impact of a mission program? Often the true impact can be quite different from the intended one or the perceived one. An honest consideration of impact opens up the possibility that there is a different yardstick for measuring mission. Frequency of meetings, or number of people served, is not sufficient. Even the hard work and fresh rapport among the leaders of mission in a congregation are only one side of the equation. The real measure of mission is how people are affected by its presence, that is, its impact.

Impact represents more than response to perceived needs, regardless of how accurate the perception. Often such perceptions are based on criteria formed externally and serve external institutional needs. But how the presence of a mission influences life in the context where it takes shape is a measure of impact. How mission is conducted, and not only its apparent outcome, becomes central. In fact mission must have two-way impact to truly be successful. Those who come to convert must in a sense be converted by what they experience. Those who come to teach must also learn. Those who come to fix and to serve must discover that they have been redirected and served in ways they could not expect. Recognition means not only discovering mutual humanity in the midst of difference; recognition means seeing "the other" as a fellow pilgrim in God's creation. Recognition means awakening to shared possibility.

The measure of mission, then, becomes cooperation. Recognition points directly toward the rise of common discernment, that is, of thinking and working together in the midst of difference. The goal is to formulate and to launch mutually agreed upon and mutually beneficial efforts to address issues of common concern, on the basis of common faith affirmation. People from North American congregations must take special, and perhaps unaccustomed, steps to suspend their cultural and institutional priorities. They must accept that in a different setting there will be different approaches to project oversight. Often, simple relationships between people who are different eclipse the impersonal, organizational style that can dominate North American thinking.

In this way recognition can extend from seeing the humanity of others to honoring the ordinary patterns of their cultures. Cooperation amid the reality of difference requires creation of an equal footing, or as equal as can possibly be established given the disparity in resources that often looms between North American congregations and people, even of the same faith, in other cultures. To move toward this equality and even to create its preconditions, a special kind of leadership is necessary. It is an adaptive leadership that looks to create new kinds of ties between people, not simply resolving conflicts or generating effective initiatives. It is a style of leadership that is focused upon mission as the creation of new ties among people, with full recognition of their differences. There has been much discussion of adaptive leadership in recent literature. In the next chapter we consider what this kind of leadership means in the face of difference.

QUESTIONS FOR DISCUSSION

What does "mission" mean to you and to the congregation you know best? What images does mission evoke, and are these favorable or unfavorable?

When have you felt closest to God? How did this occur? What could others learn from your experience?

To what extent has your congregation served as a meeting place for community groups, including people of other faiths? If this is happening, what has been the impact on the membership of the congregation?

INDIVIDUAL AND GROUP EXERCISES

1. Think of a time when you needed to ask for help. How did it feel?
2. Think of a time when you helped someone in need. How did it feel?
3. Think of a time when you formed a friendship with someone very different from you. How did it happen? How did you feel?
4. Reviewing the messages of the preceding chapters, what three things have you learned? How will you embody those things in your life? How will you share them with others?

LEARNING FROM OTHER FAITHS

At first people of different faiths seem really different. However, once you get to know them, they don't seem so different. Why?

SCRIPTURE LESSON

"He has told you, O mortal, what is good; and what does the Lord require of you but to do justice, and to love kindness, and to walk humbly with your God?" (Micah 6:8)

What does this tell us about encountering difference?

PRAY

Pray for opportunities to get to know people who are different from you—in ways that make the difference disappear.

8

LEADERSHIP FOR RECONCILIATION

We have seen that difference has become an unavoidable American reality. Religious and cultural variety of unprecedented scope is changing American communities. This reality has evoked widespread fears. An historic American instinct to restrain difference, and even instances of outright prejudice, has surfaced. Americans readily associate difference of any sort with change and threat.

For congregations as local faith communities, the issue is acute. The greatest source of fear, and one of the most obvious examples of demographic change, is the growth of Islam in the United States. Islam has evoked the most strident backlash, even instances of outright prejudice. Almost as bad, countless congregations have resisted prejudice, but seem incapable of promoting understanding and cooperation between people of different faiths. Even when faith communities and their leaders have not abetted suspicion, what have they done to eliminate it?

In this concluding chapter, I ask a basic question that reflects the course of the book's narrative: are understanding and cooperation possible in the face of difference? As I have argued, the issue is broader than tensions between Muslims and Christians and Jews. "Difference" today spans a broad spectrum of religious, cultural, social, and theological flash points. Many leaders of congregations view tensions with Islam as an issue they do not have time or resources to engage. Some even view it as a luxury they cannot afford. Instead, many congregational leaders insist, they face all-consuming internal challenges, reflecting differences over program priorities, funding, staffing, program life, and even the styles of worship and ministry they intend. To speak of "difference," it is enough for many lay and ordained persons to cite dynamics within the congregation, much less without.

To challenge this assumption, I will draw the book's threads together in two ways: first, I will describe what "leadership" must mean in congregational life today. This will be no abstract description, nor one that is one-dimensional. In the face of difference there are specific things that congregations must do to enhance their common life. Yet evidence of constructive response often is lacking. The approach to leadership can be incomplete, even seriously flawed. As congregations and their leaders well imagine, their effort to thrive has become challenging, and for some their survival may be at stake. But their instincts for how to thrive, and even survive, do not serve them well.

Second, I will argue that dealing with difference must occur within and without the congregation at the same time. Put another way, if a congregation cannot address changes in its social context, it cannot address its internal challenges. Leadership today must see the world whole, not segregating it into disconnected sectors. Unwittingly, congregational leaders may try to segregate themselves, somehow keeping the congregation isolated from its environment. But this is hardly possible. If nothing else, parishioners live in wider community circles and feel the impact of change in their civic and work and school environments. Dealing with difference is unavoidable, even as some congregations hope it will simply go away. But how can difference of various sorts be faced constructively by congregations? Which intentions are appropriate? What sort of leadership is necessary?

STRONG LEADERSHIP AND OTHER MIRAGES

It has become tiresome to hear congregations incessantly call for leadership. But the call only seems to intensify. Something vital about what congregations believe about leadership and what they experience of it seems missing. Of course, congregations are not alone. There is an energetic discussion of leadership in business, education, and government, a discussion that has continued for a generation. Across American society, leadership of appropriate and effective sorts seems in short supply. What does this discussion mean for what congregations must be and do in the face of difference?

The first thing congregational leaders and members must do is to erase some old and stubborn misconceptions. Likely the greatest of these is the image of "strong leadership." Letting go of this mirage may prove difficult. Presumably the appeal of the strong leader is clarity about core beliefs and a firm sense of direction for instilling them in the congregation. A strong leader seemingly would break through confusion, rally support, and generate fresh activity. Bringing needed energies, a strong leader would make needed things happen.

However, even an assertive, well-defined personality cannot always resolve entrenched issues. Over time, a strong leader may even add to conflict and complicate situations rather than resolving them. Some people in the congregation will be put off by the confident, forceful personality. Others will feel their preferred programs and program style are being stepped on. Still others will feel that basic tensions in the congregation have not been addressed well. Sheer activity and forceful style may actually avoid what must be faced: there are differences within and without the congregation that are not being reconciled.

If strong leadership is one mirage that congregations must discard, there is a very different leadership style where equal caution is needed. Especially at times of conflict and transition, congregations are prone to seek "pastoral" leadership. Instead of assertive firmness they seek a guide to walk them through the process of addressing difficult issues. Interim ministers especially are often charged with encouraging congregations to face nagging, unaddressed patterns in their common life.

Broadly speaking, pastoral leadership is an appealing contrast to the strong leader. Thoughtful attention to parish dynamics and to creating a process of discernment in the life of the congregation seemingly offers more promise. Even the pastoral leader, of course, must be clear about proposed direction and the proper steps to achieve it. But the pastoral leader generally will bring sensitivity to congregational life, including an appreciative grasp of its inherent strengths and possibilities. Meanwhile the pastoral leader truly ministers to the needs of parishioners as well as the dynamics of their faith community.

The appeal of pastoral leadership is both obvious and genuine. It can bring informed attention to nuance in the complex dynamics of congregational life. But there is also a subtle distraction which can beg the most important question. Pastoral leadership can reinforce a congregation's preoccupation with itself. This does not mean that existing dynamics will always be endorsed. The best pastoral leaders are alert to how things get done and how change can be encouraged. But the congregation still can be viewed as a religious system isolated from the social and religious contexts in which it sits. Even skilled pastoral leaders can miss the point this book emphasizes: difference must be faced outside and inside, or the congregation will falter. One sort of difference will not wait while another somehow is resolved.

Thus leadership can become a series of mirages that congregations pursue only to discover that they fail to deliver what is needed. The strong leader can further divide a congregation. The pastoral leader can become enmeshed in internal process and dynamics and overlook adequate attention to the full scope of difference affecting congregational life. In my opinion a congregation cannot adequately consider who it is without close attention to difference in its local context.

Of course many congregations, rightly and proudly, point to their outreach programs as evidence of vital links to the wider world. We have seen that interest in local outreach initiative has surged in recent years. It is reasonable to assume that a large percentage of American congregations have programs that benefit people beyond themselves in one way or another. In some cases, we have seen, impressive ties internationally as well as locally have emerged. Moreover much congregational outreach initiative today bypasses denominational or larger institutional channels and fund-raising alone. Much outreach initiative today involves hands-on efforts to address immediate instances of human need, including hunger, adequate housing, and response to natural disasters.

So it is inaccurate to claim that congregations generally are isolated from wider issues and contexts. There is impressive congregational proficiency at providing services for people in need. As a result, "mission"-oriented leadership is widely evident. But still there is a further step to be taken if difference is to be addressed in ways that reconcile.

Being blunt, the most enduring leadership mirage is of someone who will "take care" of things and offset the need for wider initiative. People in congregations, or any other organization for that matter, may wait for someone else to do what needs doing. A cultivated dependency can arise without notice or protest. The intrusion of dependency needs can surface in mission efforts when, with the best of intentions, congregational leaders can focus on doing things for others. Seemingly this has profound religious sanction, especially in the face of obvious human need. The issue is nuanced because in the midst of crisis or tragedy someone must step forward to act on behalf of others.

But the long-term goal of mission leadership is not to deepen dependency. The long-term goal is to free people to take initiative on their own behalf. This means, in terms of dealing with difference, that there must be emphasis not simply on doing things for people, but on doing things with people. Mission must entail producing new levels of understanding and cooperation in addressing both short-term and long-term needs. Empowering people as equals is the most desired goal. This can arise when there is full, frank attention to the internal and external circumstances of a congregation's life and its context.

Thus it is necessary to turn from misleading images of leadership and faith community toward leadership paths that are authentic and effective in facing and reconciling difference. How can this happen? Now that we have seen some leadership pitfalls, we must consider what leadership must mean for congregations now. The kind of leadership that is necessary must focus on building the capacity to work together.

A. The Leadership Congregations Must Seek

We can begin to understand leadership in general by considering one of the classic books on the subject. Now in its fifth edition, and frequently reprinted, *The Leadership Challenge* by James Kouzes and Barry Posner defines five core leadership practices.[1] In the order Kouzes and Posner consider these practices, leaders must:

1. Model the way
2. Inspire a shared vision
3. Challenge the process
4. Enable others to act
5. Encourage the heart

What implications can we draw for congregations at first blush with this list? Fortunately there are obvious touchstones. First, leadership inevitably is both personal and relational. That is, leadership is not abstract; it is a human expression embodied in people and relations among them. But given the leadership mirages we have viewed, we can see there must be an important, middle ground between the leader as a solitary figure who can alienate and the leader as one who fosters group process, and can succumb to it. It is important to note too, that most current leadership theory does not cling to old notions that leaders are rare and gifted figures. There is a broad consensus today that leaders can be educated for their tasks, though goals and styles needed to achieve them can differ widely.

Second, leaders are not simply managers of existing programs; leaders point toward fresh direction. While there are times when the leader's role is lonely and prophetic, and should be, more often leaders work to build fresh consensus, challenging inherited ways of viewing the congregation and its situation, for example. Of course, leadership must incorporate managerial functions without becoming preoccupied with them. Instead, one of the core tasks of leadership, distinguishing it from management, involves what is called "framing." That is, the leader offers a view of the organization's situation, or in this case the congregation's, that proposes a fresh way forward. An adequate frame, neither too critical nor too apologetic, can become the platform from which effective action develops.

Framing as leaders undertake it in congregations must address the reality of difference without and within. Voices and views that have not been heard must surface and must be acknowledged, however uncomfortable they and their perspective may prove. It can seem like a strain on congregational life to make difference visible, and the challenge of addressing it will be considerable. But likely such views have been swimming beneath the congregation's surface for some time, threatening to poison relations unless drawn into healthier engagement.

I emphasize that genuine leadership is more than a critique of existing ways, however apt and however thoughtfully proposed. Mere criticism can be paralyzing, however accurate and well intended. "What can we do now?" becomes the obvious response. Instead, using framing as the fulcrum, leadership can swing such discussion toward new possibilities for action. In part it can do so by the aptness of its perspective. But the most astute congregational leadership will always "encourage the heart," as Kouzes and Posner urge, though their perspective is not strictly religious. That is, genuine leadership will speak to human values and human longing, in the midst of proposing appropriate response to needs and possibilities. The leadership of a religious congregation should seek to free people to live together in better ways, so the congregation can offer a model for its context and beyond. In short, congregational leadership must remain attuned to spiritual hungers that are universally human.

Of course, what Kouzes and Posner urge about leadership can still sound theoretical and not entirely practical. Ideals can resist easy translation into the constraints of real situations. A further dip into contemporary leadership theory can sharpen the possibilities for congregations. Specifically, how can congregations that feel themselves to be "stuck," and unable to address crucial differences, take needed steps? Harvard leadership scholar Ronald Heifetz provides a crucial suggestion. His insights are all the more poignant because Heifetz has been a frequent consultant and speaker for religious leaders. He brings awareness not simply of the leadership needs of business and organizational life, but of religious America as well.

Heifetz has become the proponent for what he calls "adaptive" leadership. In all manner of organizations today, including congregations, he perceives the need for adjustment to entirely new circumstances. Old assumptions about life and work together no longer hold, and require thoughtful adaptation. For Heifetz this brings as much or more opportunity than challenge. Though change is required, organizations have the chance to clarify, and even return to, their core purpose. Basic questions must be asked because circumstances challenge assumptions.

Heifetz endorses the larger leadership message, urged by his Harvard colleague John Kotter, that leadership today requires more than technical skills. Leadership must not be confused with management. Instead, leaders must invigorate understanding of what it means for an organization to thrive. In facing new situations, it becomes central to focus on priorities. For example, what is essential to the identity and mission of an organization, and must be preserved for it to endure? On the other hand, what about an organization is the product of a bygone era and is no longer essential? The task of adaptation enables organizations to become clear about who they are and who they must become, in their actions as well as in their hearts and minds.

Crucial to our discussion, Heifetz believes that organizational adaptation requires engagement with difference. Different points of view, priorities, styles, and principles all must be surfaced and engaged appreciatively. Only in this way can new and common purpose emerge. Clearly this is not easy work. Deep-seated convictions surface, and people can feel their very selves are on trial. One of the most important tasks of the leader, Heifetz insists, is the creation of a kind of holding ground. Leaders guide the process of adaptation, helping to navigate people and organizations through disturbances as they sift through what is essential and what must be expendable. The challenge is twofold: the leader must manage herself while helping others tolerate discomfort in their circumstances, including discontent with the leader and the apparent direction being pursued.

But the truly adaptive leader consistently seeks new and appropriate ways of working together while managing people and organizations through a process of sorting out what is now needed. In this process, difference becomes central. Seemingly the obstacle, it can be engaged with sensitivity and applied to the creation of fresh consensus. The leader approaches difference with the intention of understanding and interpreting. Underlying values must be identified, astutely assessed, and probed for their formative possibilities. Above all, leaders must see that in contemporary circumstances, organizations must learn to hold multiple views in creative tension. The goal of this tension is the creation of fresh, common purpose. Multiple views need not be, and likely cannot be, reduced to one, false form of unity, as we shall discuss.

Yet another Harvard writer on leadership, Amy C. Edmondson, names the goal of the leadership congregations must pursue. In her recent book, *Teaming: How Organizations Learn, Innovate, and Compete in the Knowledge Economy*, Edmondson argues that complex organizational tasks can only be addressed cooperatively.[2] In her view, leadership must be more horizontal and shared than it is vertical and solitary. In any organization, it is not simply what one does, but with whom one pursues basic objectives.

Edmondson does not pose a new kind of structure to remake organizations for the next generation. Just the opposite, she outlines a process by which groups of people in organizations assemble to address particular tasks. When these are accomplished, they dissolve the group and reassemble in new groups for further tasks. Nor is it enough to meet and jump into action. For Edmondson the process of teaming works when two prior conditions are met: first, the team must represent difference, or it will quickly slant to a particular outlook; second, action must be built on understanding, both of the team's members and of the circumstances they face. Woven through Edmondson's description is the thought that teaming is more than response to challenge; teaming works when there is attention to shared opportunities. This can happen because of the presence of different outlooks, styles, and values. Difference is fulcrum of possibility.

The process Edmondson describes can seem risky. When people come together there must be honest conversation. The impulse to stifle divergence must be set aside. Possibilities must be sifted, and experiments must be made. There will be mistakes and course corrections. Teams doing vital work never proceed in straight lines. The process can feel messy and ambiguous. Questions must be asked. Feedback must be gained and applied honestly. Most difficult of all, group members must look to one another as resources and not as rivals. This can be paramount in the face of difference.

The goal Edmondson proposes is not just a successful result from a challenging task, only to revert to habitual forms of management. Her goal is the creation of a dynamic, new culture in the organization. This culture intends both understanding and cooperation of a new sort. It builds on insight into one another and a fresh capacity to cooperate for the common good. In this sense she, and other writers on the theme of leadership, bring much that can benefit congregations. How, in the face of difference, can congregations apply what these leadership authors suggest?

B. A Daring Goal

Throughout this book, and in the preceding discussion of leadership, a daring goal has been lurking. I have proposed that people of all sorts can find life-giving, common purpose in the midst of difference, even of the most fractious sort. I have even suggested that people seemingly divided by faith can find common ground on the basis of their own faith. One's particular beliefs and practices need not divide one from people of other faiths and practices. In fact, despite public images of faith as a realm of conflict, the goal of faith is reconciliation. Whether Jew or Muslim or Christian, or another of the great religions, the core teachings and practices point toward understanding and cooperation.

Of course the translation of this ideal into the particular circumstances of local situations is the challenge, and it is formidable. More than three hundred thousand congregations in the United States alone embody this challenge. Hopefully this book has alerted you to the nature of this challenge and has suggested ways you can begin to meet it. Now, in drawing the discussion to a close, I will draw lessons from our consideration of leadership for what congregations must be and do. Insights from leadership literature focused on the business world can be flagged for congregational application.

The first application would seem to be so obvious it needs no elaboration: congregations are faith communities and not just collections of individuals. But at a time when intensely personal spiritual journeys and a strong sense of individuality pervade American life, the core challenge is simply to create faith community. Multiple personal stories must be blended into common journey and common vocation.

The process of doing so with any success generates powerful centripetal forces. Especially now, when religious and cultural conflict is rife and society is fragmented, the impulse to pull together and ward off the wider world is profound. However, as we have seen, this impulse can go too far, even verging on fear and exclusivity. But this is hardly a valid faith expression. The challenge for congregational leaders, lay and ordained, is to develop a firm core identity rooted in faith tradition, while promoting appreciative engagement with those of other congregations or none at all.

This can happen, second, because insights from the business world reveal that difference can represent opportunity. In fact, because of faith's ideals, congregations must pay more attention to possibility than to challenge. The presence of difference means the glass is half full, not half empty. Unaddressed, difference becomes a stumbling block. Acknowledged and engaged with sensitivity, difference becomes a primary resource.

The means of making this happen begins with recalling that the basic values of the major faiths have similar contours. We have seen that love of God and love of neighbor undergird the three Abrahamic faiths, as "A Common Word" describes. Even more, common values and images pervade sacred texts and the lives toward which they point. For example, "journey" is a common theme in sacred writings and now in discussions of spirituality. The ancient figure Abraham himself embarked on a journey of faith that became a model for succeeding generations. But all major sacred figures in some manner followed both a literal and a figurative journey that was pivotal to their religious insight.

Without exception, each such journey entailed encounters with difference. More often than not these encounters both challenged assumptions and posed hurdles to be overcome, at times seemingly insuperable hurdles. But the promise of transforming difference from obstacle to opportunity can be a breathtaking step. The ancient patriarch Jacob wrestled with a mysterious figure who proved to be God; the encounter changed him decisively.

Similarly, in his book, *No Future without Forgiveness,* Desmond Tutu describes South Africa's process of creating a reconciled future.[3] It was hardly an easy journey, but focused on the Truth and Reconciliation Commission, the nation avoided what many around the world anticipated: that the end of white minority rule would launch a cycle of reprisal and counterreprisal between the races.

Something different happened in South Africa, and Archbishop Tutu has tried to encourage it broadly as he encouraged it there. As the book's title insists, people cannot move forward unless they move together. Faith cannot legitimately drive people into isolated, like-minded silos. Difference will erupt, and it is God's gift. "It is and has always been God's intention that we should live in friendship and harmony," Tutu declares. The image of the journey as a shared experience, inspired by South African example, is one hope.

Even more, Tutu hints at another theme that can build understanding and cooperation in the face of difference: "vocation." That is, on the basis of faith, we are called by God to lives of commitment individually and together. Tutu emphasizes that human beings were created by God "for togetherness, for friendship, for community, for family. . . . " In short, we are called "to live in a delicate network of interdependence." There is no movement toward God without a corresponding movement toward one another. Faith is far from complete until barriers fall.

Clearly these are ideals that leaders must teach. As we have seen in Edmondson's description of teaming, leadership involves teaching. More specifically, leaders must move people out of their heads and their hearts. The transition entails interpretation, as both Edmondson and Tutu envision. The leader must propose, and model, new and shared initiative on the basis of ideals. This is the direction of the teaming process. Different norms, views, and intentions are readily apparent. But common values and ideals lie just beneath the surface and can be tapped.

To what end does this point? Simply put, in the face of difference, and especially the presence of multiple perspectives, common purpose in the form of shared journey and vocation can arise. The role of congregations is to pursue this high calling for themselves and for their communities at the same time. The emphasis on learning is paramount and presumes its translation into action. Here learning is less an accumulation of information and more the cultivation of understanding that expands possibility. In turn, understanding points toward cooperation, for learning and activity go together.

How might this look? Imagine congregations of different faiths cooperating in a Habitat for Humanity project or a tutoring program or a homeless shelter. Imagine groups from various congregations meeting for combined scripture reading or comparisons of prayer and spirituality. Imagine jointly sponsored forums on combatting crime in the city or offering tutoring to special needs children. Imagine an interreligious forum on the economy of the region and on enhancing economic development. The possibilities for understanding and cooperation are limitless, when imagination and possibility triumph. In the process, mutual commitment to love of God and love of neighbor will become vibrant.

Congregations today bear enormous burdens. In a time of culture wars and religious pluralism, as religious institutions are diminished and disregarded, the pressure on congregations is unprecedented. In many ways they swim alone in a sea of predatory realities. But working together across lines that easily divide, congregations need no longer stand alone. When they join with one another, the promises of faith they proclaim move closer to realization. Difference is not erased, but that is not the point. Discovering the wonder and variety of God's world is the point. In the face of difference, we can behold that wonder.

QUESTIONS FOR DISCUSSION

1. Recall a time of travel to a new place, or even a move to a new home. What was the sense of challenge? What was the sense of promise?

2. Have you taken initiative to promote healing and reconciliation in your community? In your congregation or even in your family? Or at work? What was at stake? How did you proceed? What resulted?
3. What does it mean to speak of "faithful" leadership in the face of difference? Is there a distinctive style or typical goals that reflect faith in search of understanding and cooperation?

INDIVIDUAL AND GROUP EXERCISES

1. Identify two or three areas of conflict in your congregation. How has leadership been focused on these areas? What worked? To what ends?
2. How have congregations and people of faith addressed difficult civic issues in your community? Have congregations of various faiths worked together in the process? Are civic issues discussed in your congregation? What has resulted?
3. This chapter argued that leadership can view difference more as opportunity than as obstacle. Have you seen examples of this emphasis working in your setting? What can "unity" mean in practical terms for you?
4. Discuss "change" as you have experienced it in your life. Then contrast change with "adaptation" as this chapter described. When is change necessary? When is adaptation a feasible option?
5. When have you felt closest to God in the presence of people who were different from you? What did you learn? What did you have to overcome in order to learn?

LEARNING FROM OTHER FAITHS

Compare the meaning of "journey" in Christianity, Judaism, and Islam. Use major figures of each faith. What similarities become apparent and can inform your faith journey today?

SCRIPTURE LESSON

Read Deuteronomy 34: it describes Moses's climb of Mount Nebo to view the land toward which he had led the ancient Hebrew people. Today the site is a place of pilgrimage for people of the three Abrahamic faiths, each of which honors Moses. Yet recall that Moses was not able to enter the land whose pursuit had been his goal. In that sense, he did not attain the goal he pursued, yet his people did enter it. Reflect on your own journey in terms of goals pursued, some of which you have not attained. At the same time, reflect on what you learned and how you were transformed, especially if you pursued a goal in the company of other people. The story of Moses drives home the point that our lives are not defined by what we achieve, but by what we pursue and with whom we pursue them. God will not endorse just any goal, or any manner of seeking it. But when people are honored and join together, the possibility of a genuine outcome is enhanced.

PRAY

Pray for wisdom in pursing your intentions. Pray that what you seek can build a process of bringing people together for mutual benefit.

THINK ABOUT THIS DURING THE WEEK

How can you exercise leadership that unites people, at home, at work, in civic life, and in your faith community?

BIBLIOGRAPHY

CONGREGATIONAL LIFE

Becker, Penny Edgell. *Congregations in Conflict: Cultural Models of Local Religious Life*. Cambridge, UK: Cambridge University Press, 1999.

Leas, Speed B. *Discover Your Conflict Management Style*. Herndon, VA: Alban, 1998.

Oswald, Roy, and Barry Johnson. *Managing Polarities in Congregations*. Herndon, VA: Alban, 2009.

Rendle, Gil, and Alice Mann. *Holy Conversations: Strategic Planning as a Spiritual Practice for Conversations*. Herndon, VA: Alban, 2003.

Roozen, David A. "A Decade of Change in American Congregations, 2000-2010." *Faith Communities Today*. Hartford, CT: Hartford Institute for Religion Research, 2011.

Sachs, William L. *Restoring the Ties That Bind: The Grassroots Transformation of the Episcopal Church*. New York: Church Publishing, 2003.

Sachs, William L., and Michael Bos. *A Church Beyond Belief: The Search for Belonging and the Religious Future*. New York: Church Publishing, 2014.

Steinke, Peter L. *Healthy Congregations: A Systems Approach*. Herndon, VA: Alban, 2006.

INTERFAITH BACKGROUND

Armstrong, Karen. *A History of God*. New York: Ballantine, 1994.

Armstrong, Karen. *Muhammad: A Prophet for Our Time*. New York: Harper One, 2007.

Aslan, Reza. *Zealot: The Life and Times of Jesus of Nazareth*. London: Westbourne Press, 2014.

Carroll, James. *Jerusalem, Jerusalem: How the Ancient City Ignited Our Modern World*. New York: Mariner Books, 2012.

Dupuis, Jacques. *Christianity and the Religions: From Confrontation to Dialogue*. Maryknoll, NY: Orbis, 2002.

Peters, F. E. *The Children of Abraham*. Princeton, NJ: Princeton University Press, 2006.

Montefiore, Simon Sebag. *Jerusalem: The Biography*. New York: Vintage, 2012.

Ochs, Peter. *Another Reformation: Postliberal Christianity and the Jews*. Ada, MI: Baker, 2011.

Ochs, Peter. *The Return to Scripture in Judaism and Christianity*. Eugene, OR: Wipf and Stock, 2008.

Volf, Miroslav. *Allah: A Christian Response*. New York: Harper One, 2012.

ISLAM

Abdo, Genevieve. *Mecca and Main Street: Muslim Life in America after 9/11*. New York: Oxford, 2007.
Ahmed, Akbar. *Journey into America*. Washington, DC: Brookings Institution Press, 2011.
Ahmed, Akbar. *Journey into Islam*. Washington, DC: Brookings Institution Press, 2008.
Ali-Karamali, Sumbul. *The Muslim Next Door: The Qur'an, the Media, and That Veil Thing*. Ashland, OR: White Cloud Press, 2008.
Aslan, Reza. *No God But God: The Origins, Evolution, and Future of Islam*. New York: Random House, 2011.
Ayoub, Mahmoud, and Irfan A. Omar. *A Muslim View of Christianity: Essays on Dialogue*. Maryknoll, NY: Orbis, 2007.
Bin Talal, HRH Prince Ghazi bin Muhammad. *Love in the Holy Qur'an*. Chicago, IL: Kazi Publications, 2012. Free download available athttp://altafsir.com/LoveInQuranIntroEn.asp#.U8O-BbGj01o.
Coleman, Isobel. *Paradise Beneath Her Feet: How Women Are Transforming the Middle East. Council on Foreign Relations*. New York: Random House, 2013.
Esposito, John L. *What Everyone Needs to Know about Islam*. New York: Oxford, 2011.
Esposito, John L., and Dalia Mogahed, *Who Speaks for Islam?: What a Billion Muslims Really Think*. New York: Gallup Press, 2008.
Rauf, Feisal Abdul. *What's Right with Islam*. New York: Harper One, 2005.

LEADERSHIP

Cladis, George. *Leading the Team-Based Church: How Pastors and Church Staff Can Grow Together into a Powerful Fellowship of Leaders*. San Francisco: Jossey-Bass, 1999.
Edmondson, Amy C. *Teaming: How Organizations Learn, Innovate, and Compete in the Knowledge Economy*. San Francisco: Jossey-Bass, 2012.
Friedman, Edwin. *A Failure of Nerve: Leadership in the Age of the Quick Fix*. New York: Seabury, 2007.
Heifetz, Ronald A. *Leadership without Easy Answers*. Cambridge, MA: Harvard University Press, 1998.
Heifetz, Ronald A., Marty Linsky, and Alexander Grashow. *The Practice of Adaptive Leadership*. Boston: Harvard Business Review Press, 2009.
Kotter, John. *Leading Change*. Boston: Harvard Business Review Press, 2012.
Kouzes, James, and Barry Posner. *The Leadership Challenge*. 5th ed. San Francisco: Jossey-Bass, 2012.
Ochs, Peter. *Crisis, Call, and Leadership in the Abrahamic Traditions*. New York: Palgrave Macmillan, 2009.
Steinke, Peter L. *A Door Set Open: Grounding Change in Mission and Hope*. Herndon, VA: Alban, 2010.
Steinke, Peter L. *Congregational Leadership in Anxious Times*. Herndon, VA: Alban, 2006.

RECONCILIATION

Ford, David, and C. C. Pecknold, eds., *The Promise of Scriptural Reasoning*. Oxford: Wiley-Blackwell, 2006.

Bin Talal, HRH Prince Ghazi bin Muhammad, Miroslav Volf, and Melissa Yarrington, eds., *A Common Word: Muslims and Christians on Loving God and Neighbor.* Grand Rapids, MI: Eerdmans, 2009.

Knitter, Paul. *Without Buddha I Could Not Be a Christian*. 2nd ed. Croydon, UK: Oneworld Publications, 2013.

Lederach, John Paul. *The Moral Imagination: The Art and Soul of Building Peace*. New York: Oxford University Press, 2010.

Lowney, Chris. *A Vanished World: Muslims, Christians, and Jews in Medieval Spain*. New York: Oxford University Press, 2006.

Menocal, Maria. *The Ornament of the World: How Muslims, Jews, and Christians Created a Culture of Tolerance in Medieval Spain*. Boston: Back Bay Books, 2003.

Sacks, Jonathan. *The Dignity of Difference: How to Avoid the Clash of Civilizations*. New York: Bloomsbury, 2003.

Sacks, Jonathan. *To Heal a Fractured World: The Ethics of Responsibility*. New York: Schocken, 2007.

Tutu, Desmond. *God Is Not a Christian: And Other Provocations*. New York: Harper One, 2011.

Tutu, Desmond. *No Future without Forgiveness*. New York: Image Books, 2000.

Volf, Miroslav. *Exclusion and Embrace: A Theological Exploration of Identity, Otherness, and Reconciliation*. Nashville, TN: Abingdon Press, 1996.

Volf, Miroslav. *The End of Memory: Remembering Rightly in a Violent World*. Grand Rapids, MI: Eerdmans, 2006.

RELIGIOUS AND SOCIAL PLURALISM

Bishop, Bill. *The Big Sort: Why The Cloistering of Like-Minded America Is Tearing Us Apart*. New York: Houghton Mifflin Harcourt, 2008.

Davidson, Martin. *The End of Diversity as We Know It: Why Diversity Efforts Fail and How Leveraging Difference Can Succeed*. San Francisco: Berrett-Koehler, 2011.

Davis, Deborah. *Guest of Honor: Booker T. Washington, Theodore Roosevelt, and the White House Dinner That Shocked a Nation*. New York: Atria Books, 2013.

Eck, Diana. *A New Religious America*. New York: HarperSanFrancisco, 2002.

Haidt, Jonathan. *The Righteous Mind: Why Good People Are Divided by Politics and Religion*. New York: Vintage Books, 2013.

Marty, Martin E. *The One and the Many: America's Struggle for the Common Good*. Cambridge, MA: Harvard University Press, 1997.

Marty, Martin E. *When Faiths Collide*. San Francisco: Wiley-Blackwell, 2004.

NOTES

1. WHAT WOULD YOU DO?

1. Martin N. Davidson, *The End of Diversity* (San Francisco: Berrett-Koehler, 2011).

2. DIFFERENCE HITS HOME

1. Diana Eck, *A New Religious America* (New York: Harper San Francisco, 2002).

2. "Frequently Requested Statistics on Immigrants and Immigration in the United States," Migration Policy Institute, accessed 6/3/2014, http://www.migrationpolicy.org/article/frequently-requested-statistics-immigrants-and-immigration-united-states.

3. Steven A. Camarota, "Immigrants in the United States, 2010: A Profile of America's Foreign-Born Population," Center for Immigration Studies, accessed 6/3/2014, http://cis.org/2012-profile-of-americas-foreign-born-population.

4. Shifting demographics of Richmond, Virginia, are noted in the "Public Square," *Richmond Times-Dispatch*, April 10, 2011.

5. *Reflections* is a publication of Yale University Divinity School and is available at www.reflections.yale.edu.

6. David Roozen, "A Decade of Change in American Congregations, 2000 to 2010," Faith Communities Today, accessed 6/3/2014,http://faithcommunitiestoday.org/sites/faithcommunitiestoday.org/files/Decade%20of%20Change%20Final_0.pdf.

7. "Nones on the Rise." *The Pew Forum* is a publication of the Pew Research Religion and Public Life Project, accessed 6/3/2014, http://www.pewforum.org/2012/10/09/nones-on-the-rise.

8. Bill Bishop, *The Big Sort: Why the Clustering of Like-Minded America Is Tearing Us Apart* (New York: Mariner Books, 2009).

9. Polarity management is described by Roy M. Oswald and Barry Johnson, *Managing Polarities in Congregations: Eight Keys for Thriving Faith Communities* (Herndon, VA: The Alban Institute, 2010).

10. On systems approaches to congregational life, see Peter Steinke, *Congregational Leadership in Anxious Times* (Herndon, VA: The Alban Institute, 2006). Also, *Healthy Congregations: A Systems Approach* (Herndon, VA: The Alban Institute, 2006). Often seen as the articulator of systems thinking for congregations, see Edwin Friedman, *A Failure of Nerve: Leadership in the Age of the Quick Fix* (New York: Seabury Books, 2007).

3. THE GREATEST CHALLENGE

1. The Five Pillars of Islam are described in a variety of introductory texts. See, for example, John L. Esposito, *What Everyone Needs to Know about Islam* (New York: Oxford, 2011), 18–22, 58–59.

2. Various research centers document statistics on Middle East countries. For example, see "The World Factbook" of the Central Intelligence Agency, www.cia.gov. See also "Taking Stock of the Youth Challenge in the Middle East: New Data and New Questions," from the Brookings Institution, June 2010, www.brookings.edu.

3. "A Common Word" appeared as an open letter from the Muslim world to the Christian world in 2007. Two years later, its principal author and respondents assessed its impact. See Prince Ghazi bin Muhammad Bin Talal, Miroslav Volf, and Melissa Yarrington, eds., *A Common Word: Muslims and Christians on Loving God and Neighbor* (Grand Rapids, MI: Eerdmans, 2009).

4. IMAGES OF THE OTHER

1. Felicia Sonmez, "Rep. Peter King's Muslim Hearings: A Key Moment in an Angry Conversation," *Washington Post*, March 10, 2011.

2. For a description of the Know-Nothing movement, see Martin E. Marty, *Pilgrims in Their Own Land* (New York: Penguin, 1985), 274. A more

extensive treatment is found in Sydney Ahlstrom, *A Religious History of the American People* (New Haven, CT: Yale, 2004), 564–68.

5. THE CHALLENGE CONGREGATIONS MUST FACE

1. Miroslav Volf, *The End of Memory: Remembering Rightly in a Violent World* (Grand Rapids, MI: Eerdmans, 2006).

6. WHEN FASCINATION REPLACES FEAR

1. Peter Ochs, *Another Reformation: Postliberal Christianity and the Jews* (Grand Rapids, MI: Baker Academic, 2011).
2. Jonathan Haidt, *The Righteous Mind: Why Good People Are Divided By Politics and Religion* (New York: Vintage, 2013).
3. Jonathan Sacks, *The Dignity of Difference: How to Avoid the Clash of Civilizations* (New York: Bloomsbury Academic, 2003).
4. David F. Ford and C. C. Pecknold, ed., *The Promise of Scriptural Reasoning* (Malden, MA: Blackwell Publishing, 2006).

7. MISSION AND THE COMMON GOOD

1. "Called to Common Mission" is an agreement establishing full communion between the Evangelical Lutheran Church in America (ELCA) and the Episcopal Church, USA (ECUSA). Ratified by the ELCA in 1999 and ECUSA, the agreement recognizes baptisms and ordinations performed by each denomination. See a commentary on the agreement, published on February 5, 2002, at "Called to Common Mission," www.download.elca.org.
2. Robert Wuthnow, *Boundless Faith: The Global Outreach of American Churches* (Oakland, CA: University of California Press, 2010).

8. LEADERSHIP FOR RECONCILIATION

1. James Kouzes and Barry Posner, *The Leadership Challenge: How to Make Extraordinary Things Happen in Organizations*, 4th ed (San Francisco: Jossey-Bass, 2008).

2. Amy Edmondson, *Teaming: How Organizations Learn, Innovate, and Compete in the Knowledge Economy* (San Francisco: Jossey-Bass, 2012).

3. Desmond Tutu, *No Future without Forgiveness* (New York: Image Books, 2000).

ABOUT THE AUTHOR

William L. Sachs directs the Center for Interfaith Reconciliation in Richmond, Virginia. He received his PhD at the University of Chicago after earning degrees from Baylor, Vanderbilt, and Yale. He has been a visiting faculty member at various institutions, including Yale Divinity School and Seabury-Western Theological Seminary, Chicago. He currently directs the Center for Interfaith Reconciliation in Richmond, Virginia. He has written four books, including *Homosexuality and the Crisis of Anglicanism* and *Restoring the Ties That Bind.*